A Christian Delight Directed Curriculum

90 guided lessons

Book 1

By: Laura Warden

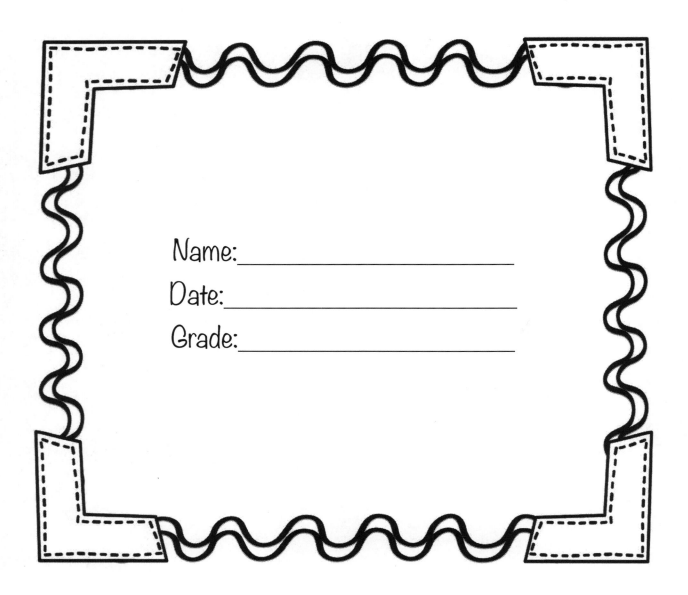

Name:_____

Date:_____

Grade:_____

Instructions

This is a delighted directed book for your creative student. Have your student choose some books. Complete 6 pages a day to complete 90 days of guided lessons. Purchase Book 2 to make it a 180 day school year. This book is a little more structured for a more well rounded education.

What you will need to complete this book

Bible

5 classic books

example(Little Women, Black Beauty, Swiss Family Robinson)

5 historical figure books

example(George Washington, Clara Barton, Christopher Columbus)

A nature book or science encyclopedia

A math curriculum of your choice

Internet Access

Pencils, erasers, gel pens, colored pencils, crayons, markers

Choose Your Books

5   Classic Novels

_____

_____

_____

_____

_____

_____

_____

5   Historical Figures

_____

_____

_____

_____

_____

_____

_____

Nature Study/Science

_____

_____

_____

Math

_____

_____

If you finish the books you chose then choose some more and write them down here._____

_____

_____

Date : _____   Day 1

Bible Time

Read for 15 min. in your bible.

Copy The Verse

For God so loved the world, that he gave his only begotten Son, that whosoever believeth in him should not perish, but have everlasting life.

John 3:16

_____

_____

_____

_____

_____

Reading and Language

Choose one of your classic novels to read.

(Read 5 pages)

Copy a paragraph from your book and circle all the nouns.

Remember a noun is a…….person, place, thing or idea!

_____

_____

_____

_____

_____

Did you put a capital letter at the beginning of your sentences and punctuation at the end?

Historical Figure Book

(Read 5 to 10 pages)

Title:_____Author:_____

Who are you reading about?

_____

Where are they from?

_____

Color the map where this person lived or lives.

A Time In History.

Apollo Moon Landing

What astronaut(s) landed on the moon?

_____

Nature Study

Draw something in nature. Write one fact about your drawing.

Math Time

Work in your math curriculum for 30 to 40 min.

Check when done. ___

Relax for a while and watch a tutorial or documentary for 30 min.

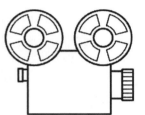 Movie Review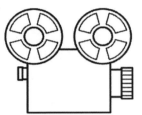

Write one thing you learned.

_____

Rate this movie. Color the stars.
5 stars mean it was Awesome!

Draw a scene from the movie.

Date : _____   Day 2

Bible Time

Read for 15 min. in your bible.

<u>Copy The Verse</u>

Trust in the Lord with all thine heart; and lean not unto thine own understanding.

Proverbs 3:5

_____

_____

_____

_____

Reading and Language

Choose one of your classic novels to read.

(Read 5 pages)

Copy a paragraph from your book and circle all the verbs.

Remember a verb is an......action word!

_____

_____

_____

_____

_____

Did you put a capital letter at the beginning of your
sentences and punctuation at the end?

Historical Figure Book

(Read 5 to 10 pages)

Title:_____Author:_____

Tell in your own words what you read today.

_____

_____

_____

_____

_____

_____

_____

_____

When did this person live or if still alive, when was this person born?

_____

A Time In History.

Independence Hall

Nature Study

Draw something in nature. Write one fact about your drawing.

_____

Math Time

Work in your math curriculum for 30 to 40 min.

Check when done. ___

Relax for a while and watch a tutorial or documentary for 30 min.

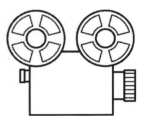
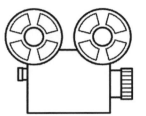

Movie Review

Write one thing you learned.

_____

Rate this movie. Color the stars.

5 stars mean it was Awesome!

Draw a scene from the movie.

Date : _____   Day 3

Bible Time

Read for 15 min. in your bible.

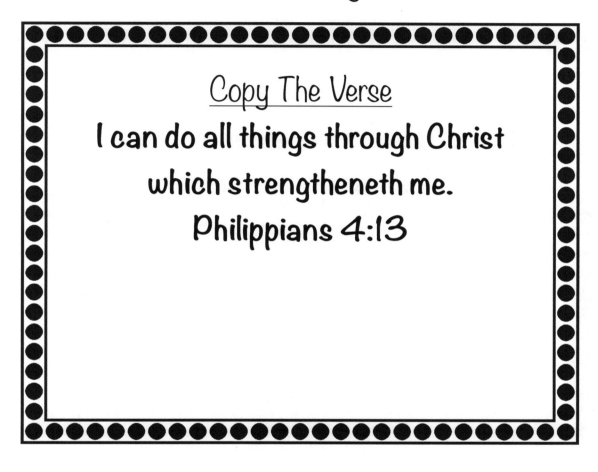

Copy The Verse

I can do all things through Christ
which strengtheneth me.
Philippians 4:13

_____

_____

_____

_____

Reading and Language

Choose one of your classic novels to read.

(Read 5 pages)

Copy a paragraph from your book and circle all the adjectives.

Remember an adjective is a......describing word!

_____

_____

_____

_____

_____

Did you put a capital letter at the beginning of your
sentences and punctuation at the end?

Historical Figure Book

(Read 5 to 10 pages)

Title:_____Author:_____

Draw a portrait of your historical figure.

A Time in History

A prairie schooner

Nature Study

Draw something in nature. Write one fact about your drawing.

_____

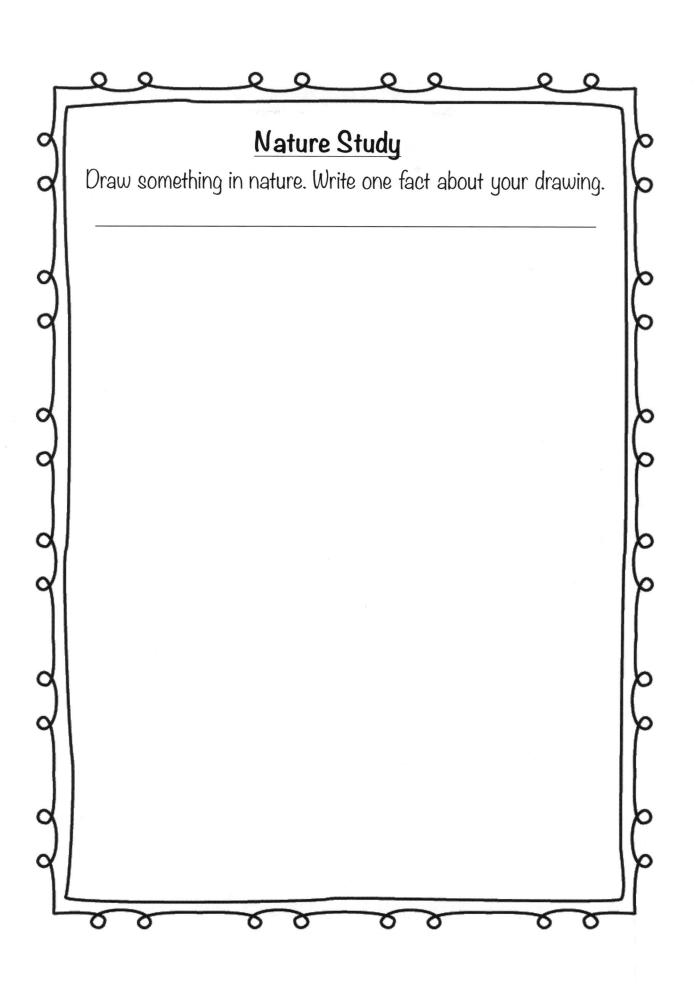

Math Time

Work in your math curriculum for 30 to 40 min.

Check when done. ___

Relax for a while and watch a tutorial or documentary for 30 min.

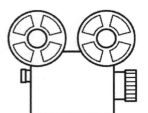 Movie Review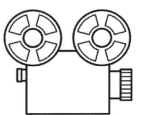

Write one thing you learned.

_____

Rate this movie. Color the stars.
5 stars mean it was Awesome!

Draw a scene from the movie.

Date : _____   Day 4

Bible Time

Read for 15 min. in your bible.

<u>Copy The Verse</u>

Be careful for nothing; but in every
thing by prayer and supplication with
thanksgiving let your requests be
made known unto God.
Philippians 4:6

_____

_____

_____

_____

Reading and Language

Choose one of your classic novels to read.

(Read 5 pages)

Copy a paragraph from your book and circle all the nouns.

Remember a noun is a......person, place, thing or idea!

_____

_____

_____

_____

_____

Did you put a capital letter at the beginning of your sentences and punctuation at the end?

Historical Figure Book

(Read 5 to 10 pages)

Title:_____Author:_____

Where does your story take place? Describe what the place looks like then draw a picture.

_____

_____

_____

_____

_____

A Time in History

Benjamin Franklin

What was Benjamin famous for?

_____

_____

Nature Study

Draw something in nature. Write one fact about your drawing.

_____

Math Time

Work in your math curriculum for 30 to 40 min.

Check when done. ___

Relax for a while and watch a tutorial or documentary for 30 min.

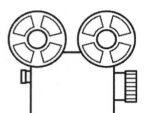 Movie Review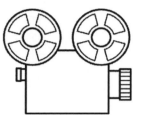

Write one thing you learned.

_____

Rate this movie. Color the stars.
5 stars mean it was Awesome!

Draw a scene from the movie.

Date : _____   Day 5

Bible Time

Read for 15 min. in your bible.

Copy The Verse

If we confess our sins, he is faithful
and just to forgive us our sins, and to
cleanse us from all unrighteousness.
1 John 1:9

_____

_____

_____

_____

Reading and Language

Choose one of your classic novels to read.

(Read 5 pages)

Copy a paragraph from your book and circle all the verbs.

Remember a verb is an......action word !

_____

_____

_____

_____

_____

Did you put a capital letter at the beginning of your
sentences and punctuation at the end?

Historical Figure Book

(Read 5 to 10 pages)

Title:_____Author:_____

What is this person famous for? Draw a picture of
what they are famous for.

_____

_____

A Time In History

George Washington was the 1st president of the
United States of America

Nature Study

Draw something in nature. Write one fact about your drawing.

_____

Math Time

Work in your math curriculum for 30 to 40 min.

Check when done. ___

Relax for a while and watch a tutorial or documentary for 30 min.

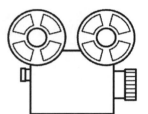 Movie Review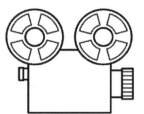

Write one thing you learned.

_____

Rate this movie. Color the stars.
5 stars mean it was Awesome!

Draw a scene from the movie.

Date : _____   Day 6

Bible Time

Read for 15 min. in your bible.

Copy The Verse

Jesus saith unto him, I am the way,
the truth, and the life: no man cometh
unto the Father, but by me.

John 14:6

_____

_____

_____

_____

Reading and Language

Choose one of your classic novels to read.

(Read 5 pages)

Copy a paragraph from your book and circle all the adjectives.

Remember an adjective is a......describing word !

_____

_____

_____

_____

_____

Did you put a capital letter at the beginning of your sentences and punctuation at the end?

Historical Figure Book

(Read 5 to 10 pages)

Title:_____Author:_____

What is the most interesting thing you learned?

_____

_____

_____

List four words to describe this person.

_____

_____

_____

_____

A Time In History

Paul Revere's Ride

What did he yell as he rode through the towns?

_____

Nature Study

Draw something in nature. Write one fact about your drawing.

_____

Math Time

Work in your math curriculum for 30 to 40 min.

Check when done. ___

Relax for a while and watch a tutorial or documentary for 30 min.

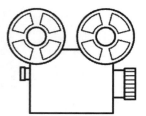 Movie Review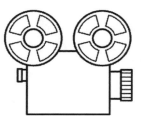

Write one thing you learned.

_____

Rate this movie. Color the stars.
5 stars mean it was Awesome!

Draw a scene from the movie.

Date : _____

Bible Time

Read for 15 min. in your bible.

Copy The Verse

But God commendeth his love toward us, in that, while we were yet sinners, Christ died for us.

Romans 5:8

_____

_____

_____

_____

_____

Reading and Language

Choose one of your classic novels to read.

(Read 5 pages)

Copy a paragraph from your book and circle all the nouns.

Remember a noun is a......person, place, thing,or idea !

_____

_____

_____

_____

_____

Did you put a capital letter at the beginning of your sentences and punctuation at the end?

Historical Figure Book

(Read 5 to 10 pages)

Title:_____Author:_____

Tell in your own words what you read.

_____

_____

_____

_____

_____

_____

_____

_____

_____

_____

A Time In History

Native Americans were a huge part of history. Name a Native American(s) that helped settlers?

_____

<u>Nature Study</u>

Draw something in nature. Write one fact about your drawing.

_____

Math Time

Work in your math curriculum for 30 to 40 min.

Check when done. ___

Relax for a while and watch a tutorial or documentary for 30 min.

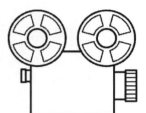 ### Movie Review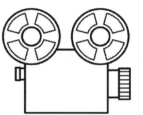

Write one thing you learned.

_____

Rate this movie. Color the stars.
5 stars mean it was Awesome!

Draw a scene from the movie.

Date :_____ Day 8

Bible Time

Read for 15 min. in your bible.

Copy The Verse

But seek ye first the kingdom of
God, and his righteousness; and all
these things shall be added unto you.

Matthew 6:33

_____

_____

_____

_____

Reading and Language

Choose one of your classic novels to read.
(Read 5 pages)
Copy a paragraph from your book and circle all the verbs.

Remember a verb is an......action word !

_____

_____

_____

_____

_____

Did you put a capital letter at the beginning of your
sentences and punctuation at the end?

Historical Figure Book

(Read 5 to 10 pages)

Title:_____Author:_____

Tell in your own words what you read.

_____

_____

_____

_____

_____

_____

_____

_____

_____

A Time In History

The Titanic

What day did the Titanic sink?

_____

Nature Study

Draw something in nature. Write one fact about your drawing.

_____

Math Time

Work in your math curriculum for 30 to 40 min.

Check when done. ___

Relax for a while and watch a tutorial or documentary for 30 min.

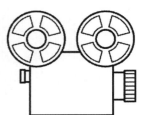 Movie Review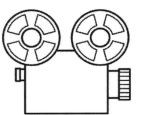

Write one thing you learned.

_____

Rate this movie. Color the stars.
5 stars mean it was Awesome!

Draw a scene from the movie.

Date : _____   Day 9

Bible Time

Read for 15 min. in your bible.

<u>Copy The Verse</u>

Come unto me, all ye that labour and
are heavy laden, and I will give you
rest.

Matthew 11:28

_____

_____

_____

_____

_____

Reading and Language

Choose one of your classic novels to read.

(Read 5 pages)

Copy a paragraph from your book and circle all the adjectives.

Remember an adjective is a......describing word !

_____

_____

_____

_____

_____

Did you put a capital letter at the beginning of your
sentences and punctuation at the end?

Historical Figure Book

(Read 5 to 10 pages)

Title:_____Author:_____

Tell me about this persons character.

_____

_____

_____

Do you think this is a person you would like to be friends with?

_____

_____

_____

_____

_____

_____

A Time In History

Model T

When was the model T car invented?

_____

Nature Study

Draw something in nature. Write one fact about your drawing.

_____

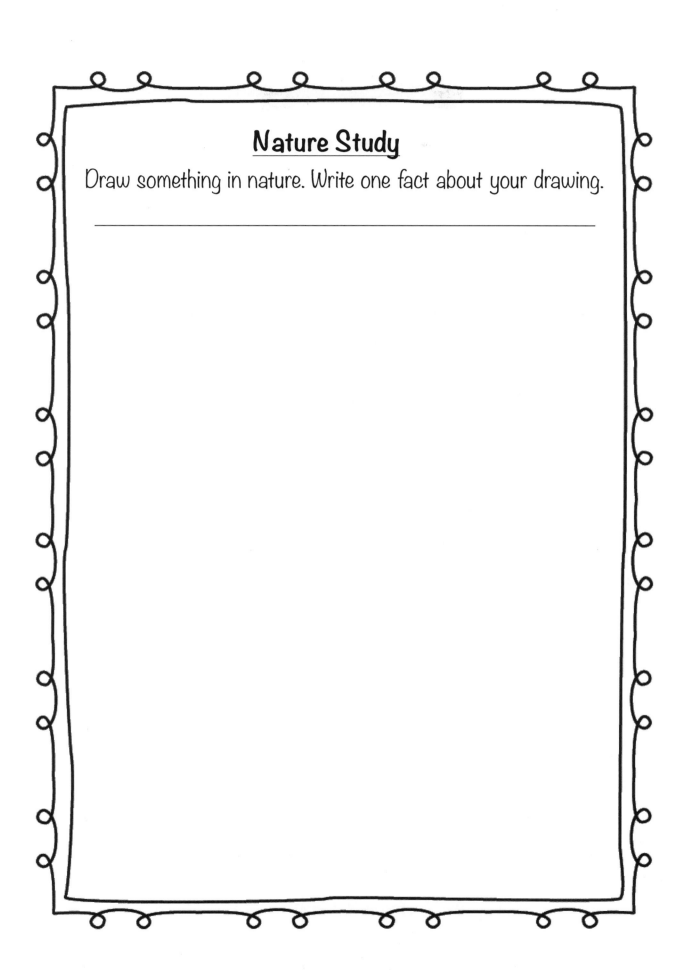

Math Time

Work in your math curriculum for 30 to 40 min.

Check when done. __

Relax for a while and watch a tutorial or documentary for 30 min.

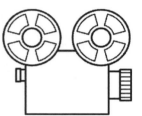 Movie Review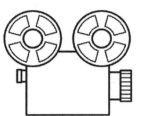

Write one thing you learned.

_____

Rate this movie. Color the stars.
5 stars mean it was Awesome!

Draw a scene from the movie.

Date : _____   Day 10

Bible Time

Read for 15 min. in your bible.

Copy The Verse

For God hath not given us the spirit of fear; but of power, and of love, and of a sound mind.

2 Timothy 1:7

_____

_____

_____

_____

Reading and Language

Choose one of your classic novels to read.

(Read 5 pages)

Copy a paragraph from your book and circle all the nouns.

Remember a noun is a......person, place, thing, or idea !

_____

_____

_____

_____

_____

Did you put a capital letter at the beginning of your sentences and punctuation at the end?

Historical Figure Book
(Read 5 to 10 pages)

Title:_____Author:_____

Do you think you could live during the time of your historical figure? Tell why or why not.

_____

_____

_____

_____

_____

_____

_____

_____

A Time In History

Abraham Lincoln

What number president was he?

_____

Nature Study

Draw something in nature. Write one fact about your drawing.

_____

Math Time

Work in your math curriculum for 30 to 40 min.

Check when done. ___

Relax for a while and watch a tutorial or documentary for 30 min.

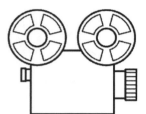 Movie Review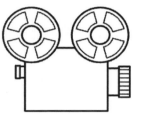

Write one thing you learned.

_____

Rate this movie. Color the stars.
5 stars mean it was Awesome!

Draw a scene from the movie.

Date : _____   Day 11

Bible Time

Read for 15 min. in your bible.

The thief cometh not, but for to steal, and to kill, and to destroy: I am come that they might have life, and that they might have it more abundantly.

John 10:10

_____

_____

_____

_____

Reading and Language

Choose one of your classic novels to read.

(Read 5 pages)

Copy a paragraph from your book and circle all the verbs.

Remember a verb is an......action word !

_____

_____

_____

_____

_____

Did you put a capital letter at the beginning of your
sentences and punctuation at the end?

Historical Figure Book

(Read 5 to 10 pages)

Title:_____Author:_____

What era is this person from?

Draw the type of clothing they wore or wear.

_____

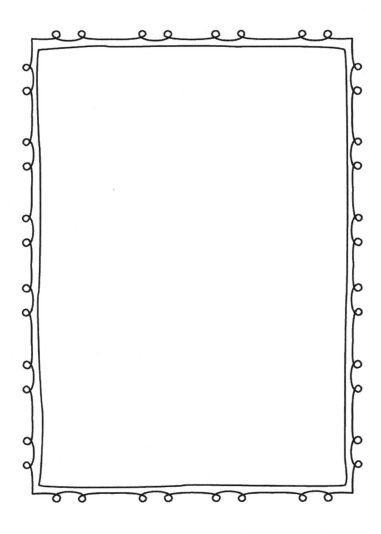

A Time In History

The Trojan Horse

What was the Trojan Horse used for?

_____

_____

Nature Study

Draw something in nature. Write one fact about your drawing.

_____

Math Time

Work in your math curriculum for 30 to 40 min.

Check when done. ___

Relax for a while and watch a tutorial or documentary for 30 min.

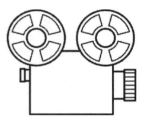 Movie Review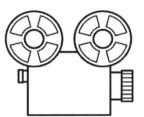

Write one thing you learned.

_____

Rate this movie. Color the stars.
5 stars mean it was Awesome!

Draw a scene from the movie.

Date : _____   Day 12

Bible Time

Read for 15 min. in your bible.

<u>Copy The Verse</u>

And the peace of God, which passeth
all understanding, shall keep your
hearts and minds through Christ
Jesus.
Philippians 4:7

_____

_____

_____

_____

_____

Reading and Language

Choose one of your classic novels to read.
(Read 5 pages)
Copy a paragraph from your book and circle all the adjectives.

Remember an adjective is a......describing word !

_____

_____

_____

_____

_____

Did you put a capital letter at the beginning of your sentences and punctuation at the end?

Historical Figure Book

(Read 5 to 10 pages)

Title:_____Author:_____

Tell in your own words what you read today.

_____

_____

_____

_____

_____

_____

_____

_____

A Time In History

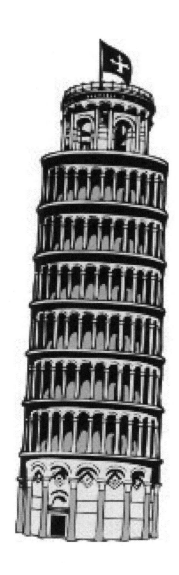

Leaning Tower Of Pisa

Why is this tower leaning?

_____

Nature Study

Draw something in nature. Write one fact about your drawing.

_____

Math Time

Work in your math curriculum for 30 to 40 min.

Check when done. ___

Relax for a while and watch a tutorial or documentary for 30 min.

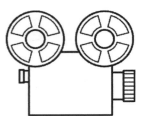 Movie Review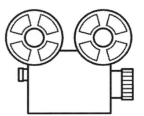

Write one thing you learned.

_____

Rate this movie. Color the stars.
5 stars mean it was Awesome!

Draw a scene from the movie.

Date : _____   Day 13

Bible Time

Read for 15 min. in your bible.

Continue to practice copy work. Choose a verse in the Bible that you read today that spoke to your heart. Copy it on the lines below.

_____

_____

_____

_____

Reading and Language

Choose one of your classic novels to read.

(Read 5 pages)

Copy a paragraph from your book and circle all the nouns.

Remember a noun is a......person, place, thing, or idea !

_____

_____

_____

_____

_____

Did you put a capital letter at the beginning of your sentences and punctuation at the end?

Historical Figure Book

(Read 5 to 10 pages)

Title:_____Author:_____

Did this person face any struggles during their life if so what were the struggles?

_____

_____

_____

_____

_____

How did they over come their struggles?

_____

_____

_____

_____

A Time In History

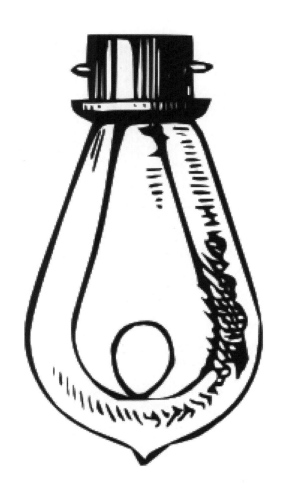

The Lightbulb
Who invented the lightbulb?

_____

Nature Study

Draw something in nature. Write one fact about your drawing.

_____

Math Time

Work in your math curriculum for 30 to 40 min.

Check when done. ___

Relax for a while and watch a tutorial or documentary for 30 min.

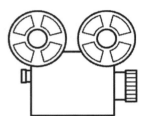 Movie Review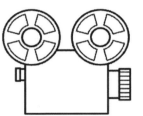

Write one thing you learned.

_____

Rate this movie. Color the stars.
5 stars mean it was Awesome!

Draw a scene from the movie.

Date : _____   Day 13

Bible Time

Read for 15 min. in your bible.

Continue to practice copy work. Choose a verse in the Bible that you read today that spoke to your heart. Copy it on the lines below.

_____

_____

_____

_____

_____

Reading and Language

Choose one of your classic novels to read.
(Read 5 pages)
Copy a paragraph from your book and circle all the verbs.

Remember a verb is an......action word !

_____

_____

_____

_____

_____

Did you put a capital letter at the beginning of your
sentences and punctuation at the end?

Historical Figure Book

(Read 5 to 10 pages)

Title:_____Author:_____

Tell about this persons education. Did they go to school? Draw a picture of what school might have looked like for them.

_____

_____

_____

_____

A Time In History

A Suit of Armor

What era is this soldier from?

_____

Nature Study

Draw something in nature. Write one fact about your drawing.

_____

Math Time

Work in your math curriculum for 30 to 40 min.

Check when done. ___

Relax for a while and watch a tutorial or documentary for 30 min.

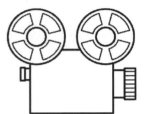 Movie Review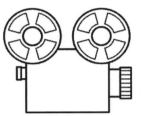

Write one thing you learned.

_____

Rate this movie. Color the stars.
5 stars mean it was Awesome!

Draw a scene from the movie.

Date :_____   Day 14

Bible Time

Read for 15 min. in your bible.

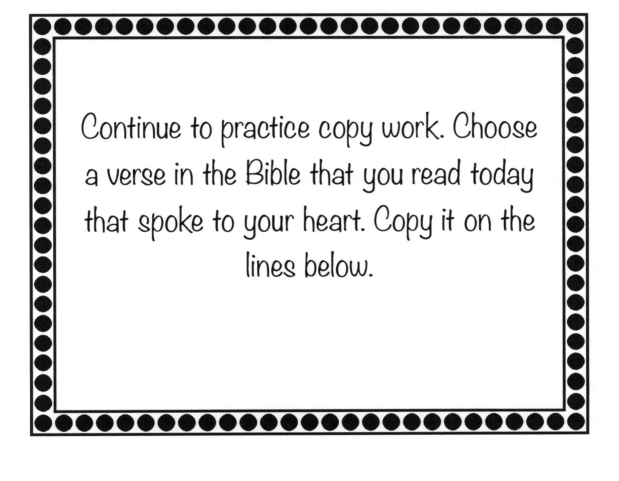

Continue to practice copy work. Choose a verse in the Bible that you read today that spoke to your heart. Copy it on the lines below.

_____

_____

_____

_____

Reading and Language

Choose one of your classic novels to read.

(Read 5 pages)

Copy a paragraph from your book and circle all the adjectives.

Remember an adjective is a......describing word !

_____

_____

_____

_____

_____

Did you put a capital letter at the beginning of your sentences and punctuation at the end?

Historical Figure Book

(Read 5 to 10 pages)

Title:_____Author:_____

Draw a picture of a scene from your book.

A Time In History

Queen Victoria

She was queen of the United Kingdom of Great
Britain and Ireland

Nature Study

Draw something in nature. Write one fact about your drawing.

_____

Math Time

Work in your math curriculum for 30 to 40 min.

Check when done. ___

Relax for a while and watch a tutorial or documentary for 30 min.

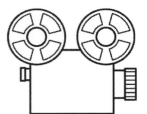 Movie Review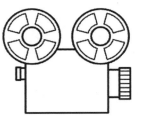

Write one thing you learned.

_____

Rate this movie. Color the stars.

5 stars mean it was Awesome!

Draw a scene from the movie.

Bible Time

Read for 15 min. in your bible.

Continue to practice copy work. Choose a verse in the Bible that you read today that spoke to your heart. Copy it on the lines below.

_____

_____

_____

_____

Reading and Language

Choose one of your classic novels to read.
(Read 5 pages)
Copy a paragraph from your book and circle all the nouns.

Remember a noun is a......person, place, thing or idea !

_____

_____

_____

_____

_____

Did you put a capital letter at the beginning of your
sentences and punctuation at the end?

Historical Figure Book

(Read 5 to 10 pages)

Title:_____Author:_____

If you could ask this person anything what would you ask?

_____

_____

Design a postage stamp in honor of this person.

A Time In History

Stonehenge

Where is Stonehenge located?

_____

Nature Study

Draw something in nature. Write one fact about your drawing.

_____

Math Time

Work in your math curriculum for 30 to 40 min.

Check when done. ___

Relax for a while and watch a tutorial or documentary for 30 min.

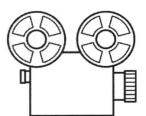

Movie Review

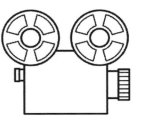

Write one thing you learned.

_____

Rate this movie. Color the stars.
5 stars mean it was Awesome!

Draw a scene from the movie.

Bible Time

Read for 15 min. in your bible.

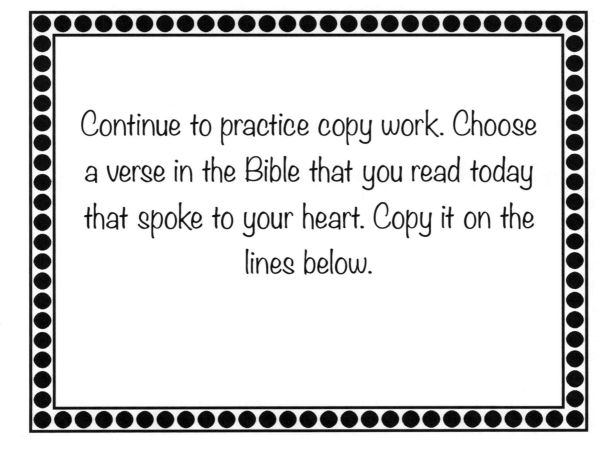

Continue to practice copy work. Choose a verse in the Bible that you read today that spoke to your heart. Copy it on the lines below.

_____

_____

_____

_____

_____

Reading and Language

Choose one of your classic novels to read.
(Read 5 pages)
Copy a paragraph from your book and circle all the verbs.

Remember a verb is an......action word !

_____

_____

_____

_____

_____

Did you put a capital letter at the beginning of your
sentences and punctuation at the end?

Historical Figure Book

(Read 5 to 10 pages)

Title:_____Author:_____

Tell in your own words what you read today.

_____

_____

_____

_____

_____

_____

_____

_____

A Time In History

The Mayflower

When did the Mayflower sail for the new world?

_____

Nature Study

Draw something in nature. Write one fact about your drawing.

_____

Math Time

Work in your math curriculum for 30 to 40 min.

Check when done. ___

Relax for a while and watch a tutorial or documentary for 30 min.

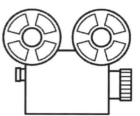 Movie Review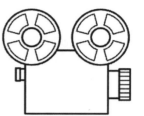

Write one thing you learned.

_____

Rate this movie. Color the stars.
5 stars mean it was Awesome!

Draw a scene from the movie.

Date :_____   Day 17

Bible Time

Read for 15 min. in your bible.

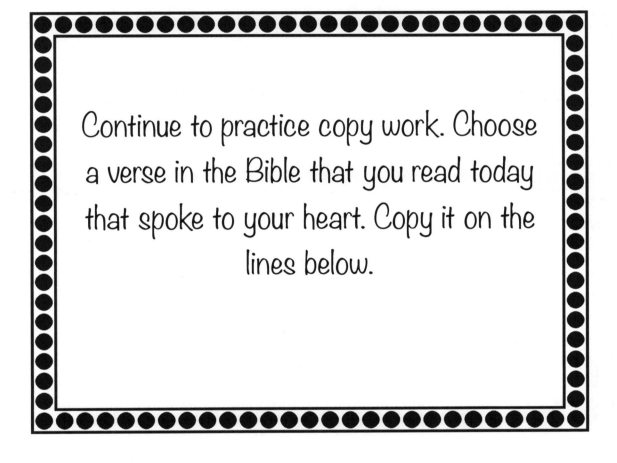

Continue to practice copy work. Choose a verse in the Bible that you read today that spoke to your heart. Copy it on the lines below.

_____

_____

_____

_____

Reading and Language

Choose one of your classic novels to read.

(Read 5 pages)

Copy a paragraph from your book and circle all the adjectives.

Remember an adjective is a......describing word !

_____

_____

_____

_____

_____

Did you put a capital letter at the beginning of your sentences and punctuation at the end?

Historical Figure Book
(Read 5 to 10 pages)

Title:_____Author:_____

How did this person die? Or if still alive what are they doing now?

_____

_____

_____

_____

_____

_____

_____

Draw a picture.

A Time In History

President Roosevelt

Theodore Roosevelt was the 26th president of the United State of America

Nature Study

Draw something in nature. Write one fact about your drawing.

_____

Math Time

Work in your math curriculum for 30 to 40 min.

Check when done. ___

Relax for a while and watch a tutorial or documentary for 30 min.

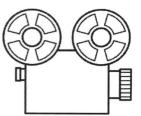
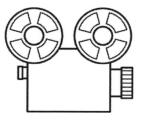

Movie Review

Write one thing you learned.

_____

Rate this movie. Color the stars.
5 stars mean it was Awesome!

Draw a scene from the movie.

Date :_____   Day 18

Bible Time

Read for 15 min. in your bible.

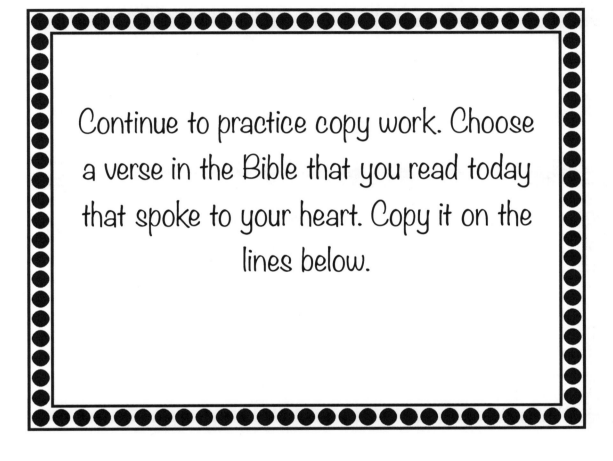

Continue to practice copy work. Choose a verse in the Bible that you read today that spoke to your heart. Copy it on the lines below.

_____

_____

_____

_____

_____

Reading and Language

Choose one of your classic novels to read.

(Read 5 pages)

Copy a paragraph from your book and circle all the nouns.

Remember a noun is a......person, place, thing or idea !

_____

_____

_____

_____

_____

Did you put a capital letter at the beginning of your
sentences and punctuation at the end?

Historical Figure Book

(Read 5 to 10 pages)

Title:_____Author:_____

Did you like learning about this person?
Tell why or why not.

_____

_____

_____

_____

_____

_____

_____

_____

_____

_____

A Time In History

Clara Barton

Clara Barton was a nurse during the civil war.

Nature Study

Draw something in nature. Write one fact about your drawing.

_____

Math Time

Work in your math curriculum for 30 to 40 min.

Check when done. ___

Relax for a while and watch a tutorial or documentary for 30 min.

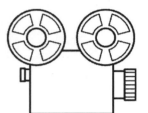 Movie Review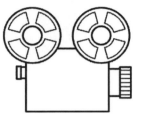

Write one thing you learned.

_____

Rate this movie. Color the stars.
5 stars mean it was Awesome!

Draw a scene from the movie.

Bible Time

Read for 15 min. in your bible.

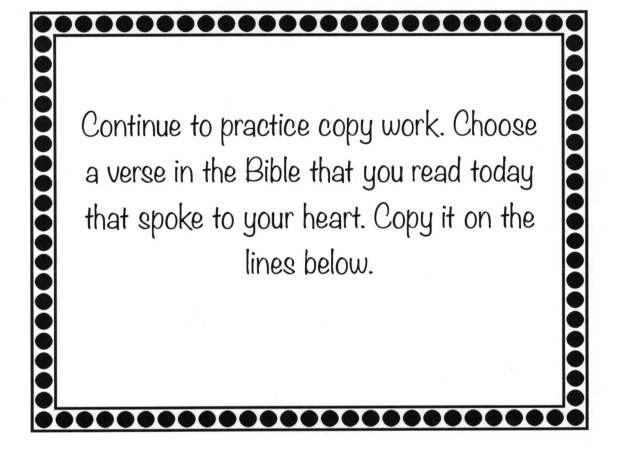

Continue to practice copy work. Choose a verse in the Bible that you read today that spoke to your heart. Copy it on the lines below.

_____

_____

_____

_____

Reading and Language

Choose one of your classic novels to read.

(Read 5 pages)

Copy a paragraph from your book and circle all the verbs.

Remember a verb is an......action word !

_____

_____

_____

_____

_____

Did you put a capital letter at the beginning of your sentences and punctuation at the end?

Historical Figure Book

(Read 5 to 10 pages)

Title:_____Author:_____

Would you recommend this book to someone else?
Tell why you would recommend it.

_____

_____

_____

_____

_____

_____

_____

_____

_____

A Time In History

Roman Colosseum

What was the colosseum used for?

_____

_____

Nature Study

Draw something in nature. Write one fact about your drawing.

_____

Math Time

Work in your math curriculum for 30 to 40 min.

Check when done. ___

Relax for a while and watch a tutorial or documentary for 30 min.

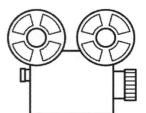

Movie Review

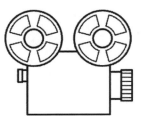

Write one thing you learned.

_____

Rate this movie. Color the stars.
5 stars mean it was Awesome!

Draw a scene from the movie.

Date :_____   Day 20

Bible Time

Read for 15 min. in your bible.

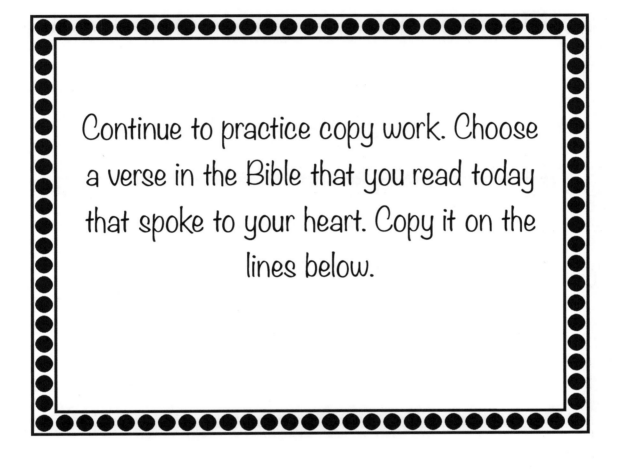

Continue to practice copy work. Choose
a verse in the Bible that you read today
that spoke to your heart. Copy it on the
lines below.

_____

_____

_____

_____

Reading and Language

Choose one of your classic novels to read.
(Read 5 pages)
Copy a paragraph from your book and circle all the adjectives.

Remember an adjective is a.....describing word !

_____

_____

_____

_____

_____

Did you put a capital letter at the beginning of your
sentences and punctuation at the end?

History

Were you inspired by your historical figure book? If you could do anything in the world what would you do?

_____

_____

_____

_____

_____

Draw a picture of what you would do.

A Time In History

A Catapult

What was a catapult used for?

_____

When was a catapult used?

_____

Nature Study

Draw something in nature. Write one fact about your drawing.

_____

Math Time

Work in your math curriculum for 30 to 40 min.

Check when done. ___

Relax for a while and watch a tutorial or documentary for 30 min.

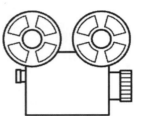

Movie Review

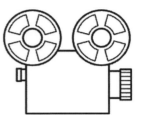

Write one thing you learned.

_____

Rate this movie. Color the stars.

5 stars mean it was Awesome!

Draw a scene from the movie.

Date :_____   Day 21

Bible Time

Read for 15 min. in your bible.

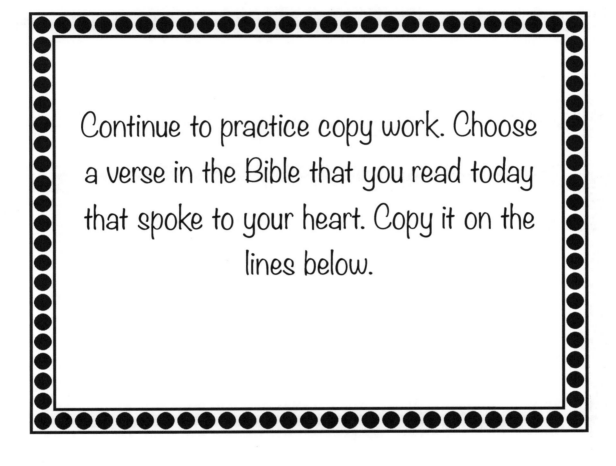

Continue to practice copy work. Choose a verse in the Bible that you read today that spoke to your heart. Copy it on the lines below.

_____

_____

_____

_____

_____

Reading and Language

Choose one of your classic novels to read.

(Read 5 pages)

Copy a paragraph from your book and circle all the nouns.

Remember a noun is a......person, place, thing or idea !

Did you put a capital letter at the beginning of your sentences and punctuation at the end?

Historical Figure Book

(Read 5 to 10 pages)

Title:_____Author:_____

Who are you reading about?

_____

Where are they from?

_____

Color the map where this person lived or lives.

A Time In History

Francis Scott Key
What song did he write?

_____

Nature Study

Draw something in nature. Write one fact about your drawing.

_____

Math Time

Work in your math curriculum for 30 to 40 min.

Check when done. ___

Relax for a while and watch a tutorial or documentary for 30 min.

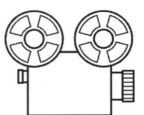 Movie Review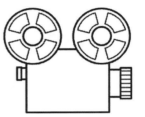

Write one thing you learned.

Rate this movie. Color the stars.
5 stars mean it was Awesome!

Draw a scene from the movie.

Date :_____   Day 22

<u>Bible Time</u>

Read for 15 min. in your bible.

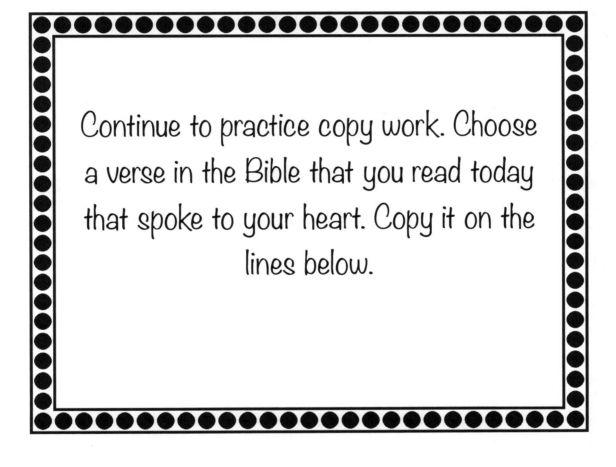

Continue to practice copy work. Choose
a verse in the Bible that you read today
that spoke to your heart. Copy it on the
lines below.

_____

_____

_____

_____

Reading and Language

Choose one of your classic novels to read.

(Read 5 pages)

Copy a paragraph from your book and circle all the verbs.

Remember a verb is an......action word !

_____

_____

_____

_____

_____

Did you put a capital letter at the beginning of your sentences and punctuation at the end?

Historical Figure Book

(Read 5 to 10 pages)

Title:_____Author:_____

Tell in your own words what you read today.

_____

_____

_____

_____

_____

_____

_____

When did this person live or if still alive, when was this person born?

_____

A Time In History

John Smith

This explorer was once saved by an Indian princess,
what was the name of the princess?

_____

Nature Study

Draw something in nature. Write one fact about your drawing.

_____

Math Time

Work in your math curriculum for 30 to 40 min.

Check when done. ___

Relax for a while and watch a tutorial or documentary for 30 min.

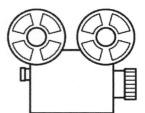 Movie Review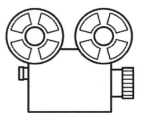

Write one thing you learned.

_____

Rate this movie. Color the stars.
5 stars mean it was Awesome!

Draw a scene from the movie.

Date : _____   Day 23

Bible Time

Read for 15 min. in your bible.

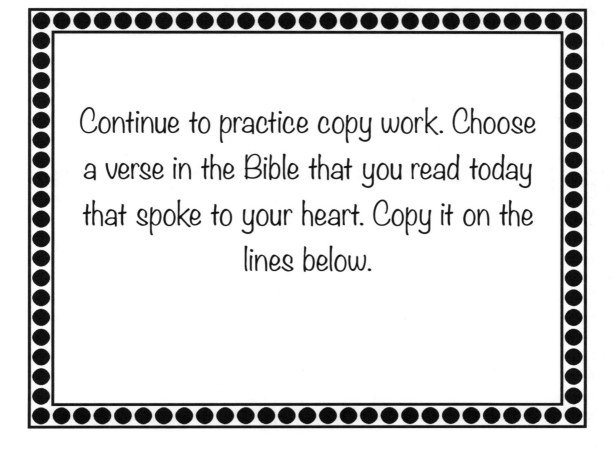

Continue to practice copy work. Choose a verse in the Bible that you read today that spoke to your heart. Copy it on the lines below.

_____

_____

_____

_____

_____

Reading and Language

Choose one of your classic novels to read.
(Read 5 pages)
Copy a paragraph from your book and circle all the adjectives.

Remember an adjective is a.....describing word !

_____

_____

_____

_____

_____

Did you put a capital letter at the beginning of your
sentences and punctuation at the end?

Historical Figure Book

(Read 5 to 10 pages)

Title:_____Author:_____

Draw a portrait of your historical figure.

A Time In History

Gold Rush

When was the gold rush?

_____

Nature Study

Draw something in nature. Write one fact about your drawing.

_____

Math Time

Work in your math curriculum for 30 to 40 min.

Check when done. ___

Relax for a while and watch a tutorial or documentary for 30 min.

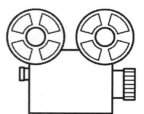 Movie Review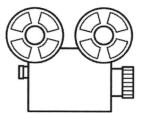

Write one thing you learned.

_____

Rate this movie. Color the stars.
5 stars mean it was Awesome!

Draw a scene from the movie.

Date :_____   Day 24

Bible Time

Read for 15 min. in your bible.

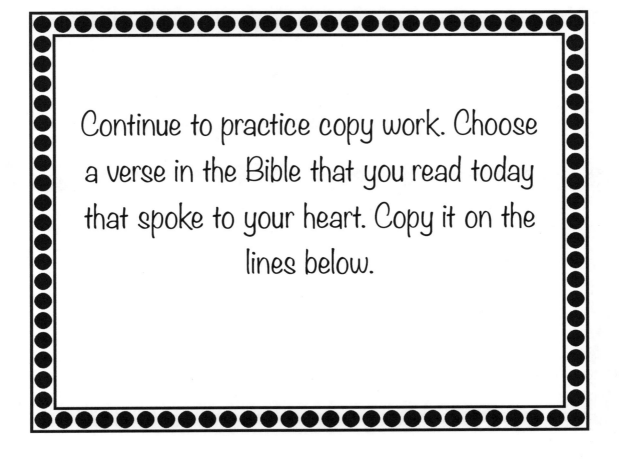

Continue to practice copy work. Choose
a verse in the Bible that you read today
that spoke to your heart. Copy it on the
lines below.

_____

_____

_____

_____

_____

Reading and Language

Choose one of your classic novels to read.

(Read 5 pages)

Copy a paragraph from your book and circle all the nouns.

Remember a noun is a......person,place,thing, or idea !

_____

_____

_____

_____

_____

Did you put a capital letter at the beginning of your
sentences and punctuation at the end?

Historical Figure Book

(Read 5 to 10 pages)

Title:_____Author:_____

Where does your story take place? Describe what the place looks like then draw a picture.

_____

_____

_____

_____

_____

A Time In History

Minute Men

What are minute men?

_____

_____

Nature Study

Draw something in nature. Write one fact about your drawing.

_____

Math Time

Work in your math curriculum for 30 to 40 min.

Check when done. ___

Relax for a while and watch a tutorial or documentary for 30 min.

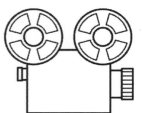 Movie Review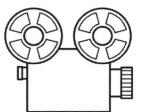

Write one thing you learned.

_____

Rate this movie. Color the stars.

5 stars mean it was Awesome!

Draw a scene from the movie.

Date : _____

Bible Time

Read for 15 min. in your bible.

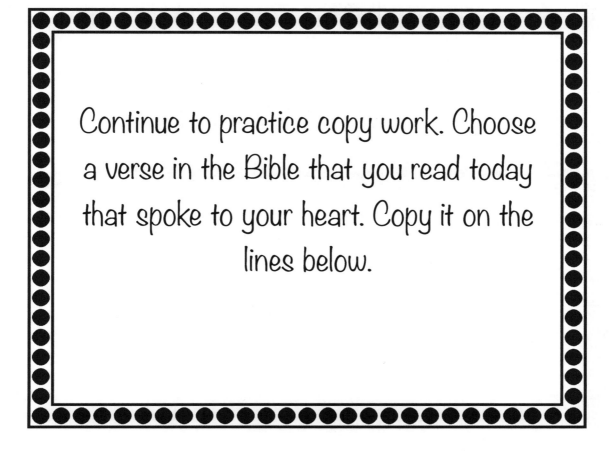

Continue to practice copy work. Choose a verse in the Bible that you read today that spoke to your heart. Copy it on the lines below.

_____

_____

_____

_____

_____

Reading and Language

Choose one of your classic novels to read.

(Read 5 pages)

Copy a paragraph from your book and circle all the verbs.

Remember a verb is an......action word !

_____

_____

_____

_____

_____

Did you put a capital letter at the beginning of your sentences and punctuation at the end?

Historical Figure Book

(Read 5 to 10 pages)

Title:_____Author:_____

What is this person famous for?Draw a picture of
what they are famous for.

_____

_____

A Time In History

Discovery Of America

Who discovered America and what year was it discovered?

_____

Nature Study

Draw something in nature. Write one fact about your drawing.

_____

Math Time

Work in your math curriculum for 30 to 40 min.

Check when done. ___

Relax for a while and watch a tutorial or documentary for 30 min.

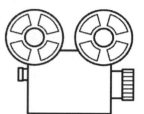 Movie Review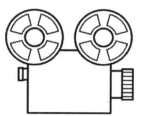

Write one thing you learned.

_____

Rate this movie. Color the stars.
5 stars mean it was Awesome!

Draw a scene from the movie.

Date :_____   Day 26

Bible Time

Read for 15 min. in your bible.

Continue to practice copy work. Choose a verse in the Bible that you read today that spoke to your heart. Copy it on the lines below.

_____

_____

_____

_____

Reading and Language

Choose one of your classic novels to read.

(Read 5 pages)

Copy a paragraph from your book and circle all the adjectives.

Remember an adjective is a......describing word !

_____

_____

_____

_____

_____

Did you put a capital letter at the beginning of your sentences and punctuation at the end?

Historical Figure Book

(Read 5 to 10 pages)

Title:_____Author:_____

What is the most interesting thing you learned?

_____

_____

_____

List four words to describe this person.

_____

_____

_____

_____

A Time In History

Joan of Arc

Joan of Arc was a martyr, saint and military leader during the hundred year war.

Nature Study

Draw something in nature. Write one fact about your drawing.

_____

Math Time

Work in your math curriculum for 30 to 40 min.

Check when done. ___

Relax for a while and watch a tutorial or documentary for 30 min.

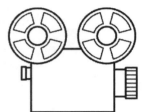 <u>Movie Review</u>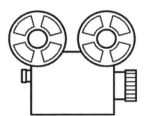

Write one thing you learned.

_____

Rate this movie. Color the stars.
5 stars mean it was Awesome!

Draw a scene from the movie.

Date : _____   Day 27

Bible Time

Read for 15 min. in your bible.

Continue to practice copy work. Choose a verse in the Bible that you read today that spoke to your heart. Copy it on the lines below.

_____

_____

_____

_____

Reading and Language

Choose one of your classic novels to read.

(Read 5 pages)

Copy a paragraph from your book and circle all the nouns.

Remember a noun is a......person,place,thing, or idea !

_____

_____

_____

_____

_____

Did you put a capital letter at the beginning of your sentences and punctuation at the end?

Historical Figure Book

(Read 5 to 10 pages)

Title:_____Author:_____

Tell in your own words what you read.

_____

_____

_____

_____

_____

_____

_____

_____

_____

_____

A Time In History

Painter Leonardo da Vinci

What famous painting did he paint?

_____

Nature Study

Draw something in nature. Write one fact about your drawing.

_____

Math Time

Work in your math curriculum for 30 to 40 min.

Check when done. ___

Relax for a while and watch a tutorial or documentary for 30 min.

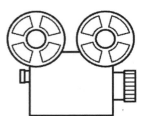 <u>Movie Review</u>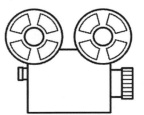

Write one thing you learned.

_____

Rate this movie. Color the stars.
5 stars mean it was Awesome!

Draw a scene from the movie.

Date :_____   Day 28

Bible Time

Read for 15 min. in your bible.

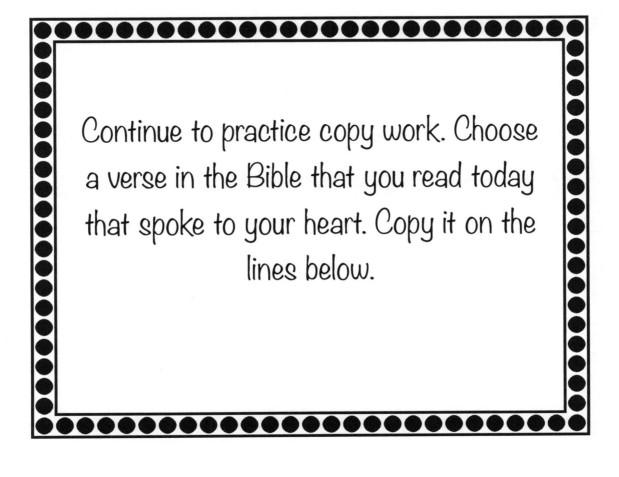

Continue to practice copy work. Choose
a verse in the Bible that you read today
that spoke to your heart. Copy it on the
lines below.

_____

_____

_____

_____

Reading and Language

Choose one of your classic novels to read.

(Read 5 pages)

Copy a paragraph from your book and circle all the verbs.

Remember a verb is an......action word !

_____

_____

_____

_____

_____

Did you put a capital letter at the beginning of your
sentences and punctuation at the end?

Historical Figure Book

(Read 5 to 10 pages)

Title:_____Author:_____

Tell in your own words what you read.

_____

_____

_____

_____

_____

_____

_____

_____

_____

_____

A Time In History

Battle at Bunker Hill

What war was the Battle at Bunker Hill?

_____

Nature Study

Draw something in nature. Write one fact about your drawing.

_____

Math Time

Work in your math curriculum for 30 to 40 min.

Check when done. ___

Relax for a while and watch a tutorial or documentary for 30 min.

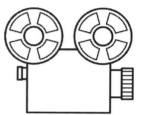 Movie Review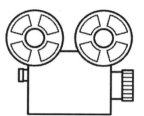

Write one thing you learned.

_____

Rate this movie. Color the stars.
5 stars mean it was Awesome!

Draw a scene from the movie.

Date : _____

Bible Time

Read for 15 min. in your bible.

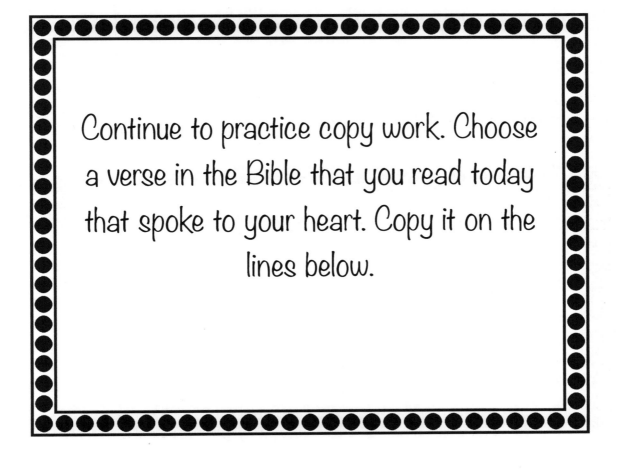

Continue to practice copy work. Choose a verse in the Bible that you read today that spoke to your heart. Copy it on the lines below.

_____

_____

_____

_____

_____

Reading and Language

Choose one of your classic novels to read.
(Read 5 pages)
Copy a paragraph from your book and circle all the adjectives.

Remember an adjective is a......describing word !

_____

_____

_____

_____

_____

Did you put a capital letter at the beginning of your
sentences and punctuation at the end?

Historical Figure Book

(Read 5 to 10 pages)

Title:_____Author:_____

Tell me about this persons character.

_____

_____

_____

Do you think this is a person you would like to be friends with?

_____

_____

_____

_____

_____

A Time In History

Drummer Boy

What war do you think he is from?

_____

Nature Study

Draw something in nature. Write one fact about your drawing.

_____

Math Time

Work in your math curriculum for 30 to 40 min.

Check when done. ___

Relax for a while and watch a tutorial or documentary for 30 min.

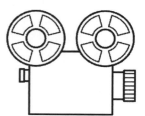 Movie Review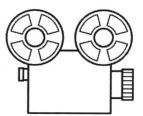

Write one thing you learned.

_____

Rate this movie. Color the stars.
5 stars mean it was Awesome!

Draw a scene from the movie.

Date :_____   Day 30

Bible Time

Read for 15 min. in your bible.

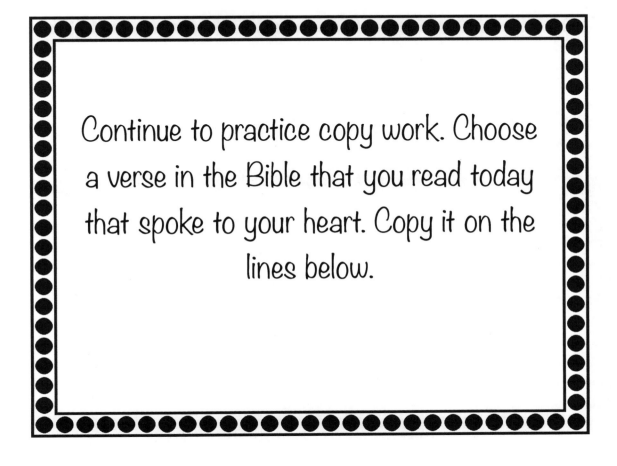

Continue to practice copy work. Choose a verse in the Bible that you read today that spoke to your heart. Copy it on the lines below.

_____

_____

_____

_____

Reading and Language

Choose one of your classic novels to read.

(Read 5 pages)

Copy a paragraph from your book and circle all the nouns.

Remember a noun is a......person,place,thing, or idea !

_____

_____

_____

_____

_____

Did you put a capital letter at the beginning of your
sentences and punctuation at the end?

Historical Figure Book

Title:_____Author:_____

Do you think you could live during the time of your
historical figure? Tell why or why not.

_____

_____

_____

_____

_____

_____

_____

_____

_____

A Time In History

Transcontinental Railroad

May 10,1869 the Transcontinental Railroad was completed.

Nature Study

Draw something in nature. Write one fact about your drawing.

_____

Math Time

Work in your math curriculum for 30 to 40 min.

Check when done. ___

Relax for a while and watch a tutorial or documentary for 30 min.

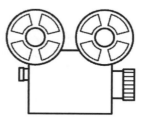 Movie Review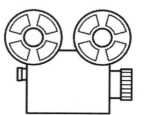

Write one thing you learned.

Rate this movie. Color the stars.
5 stars mean it was Awesome!

Draw a scene from the movie.

Bible Time

Read for 15 min. in your bible.

Continue to practice copy work. Choose
a verse in the Bible that you read today
that spoke to your heart. Copy it on the
lines below.

_____

_____

_____

_____

Reading and Language

Choose one of your classic novels to read.
(Read 5 pages)
Copy a paragraph from your book and circle all the verbs.

Remember a verb is an......action word !

_____

_____

_____

_____

_____

Did you put a capital letter at the beginning of your
sentences and punctuation at the end?

Historical Figure Book

(Read 5 to 10 pages)

Title:_____Author:_____

What era is this person from?

Draw the type of clothing they wore or wear.

_____

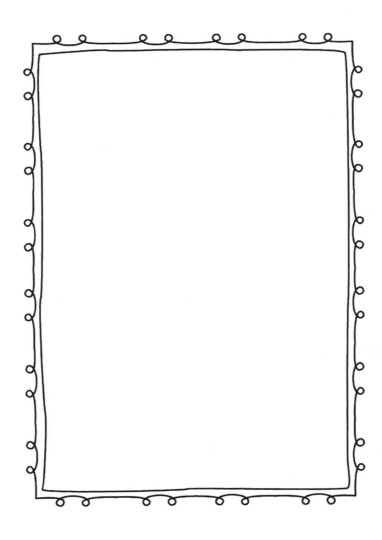

A Time In History

Sphinx of Giza
It Is the oldest known monumental sculpture in Egypt.

Nature Study

Draw something in nature. Write one fact about your drawing.

_____

Math Time

Work in your math curriculum for 30 to 40 min.

Check when done. ___

Relax for a while and watch a tutorial or documentary for 30 min.

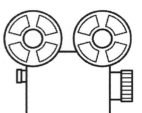 Movie Review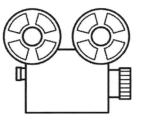

Write one thing you learned.

_____

Rate this movie. Color the stars.
5 stars mean it was Awesome!

Draw a scene from the movie.

Date : _____

Bible Time

Read for 15 min. in your bible.

Continue to practice copy work. Choose a verse in the Bible that you read today that spoke to your heart. Copy it on the lines below.

_____

_____

_____

_____

Reading and Language

Choose one of your classic novels to read.
(Read 5 pages)

Copy a paragraph from your book and circle all the adjectives.

Remember an adjective is a......describing word !

_____

_____

_____

_____

_____

Did you put a capital letter at the beginning of your
sentences and punctuation at the end?

Historical Figure Book

(Read 5 to 10 pages)

Title:_____Author:_____

Tell in your own words what you read today.

_____

_____

_____

_____

_____

_____

_____

_____

_____

A Time In History

The Liberty Bell

What is engraved on the side of the Liberty Bell?

_____

_____

Nature Study

Draw something in nature. Write one fact about your drawing.

_____

Math Time

Work in your math curriculum for 30 to 40 min.

Check when done. ___

Relax for a while and watch a tutorial or documentary for 30 min.

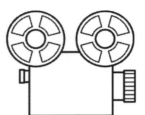 Movie Review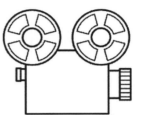

Write one thing you learned.

_____

Rate this movie. Color the stars.

5 stars mean it was Awesome!

Draw a scene from the movie.

Bible Time

Read for 15 min. in your bible.

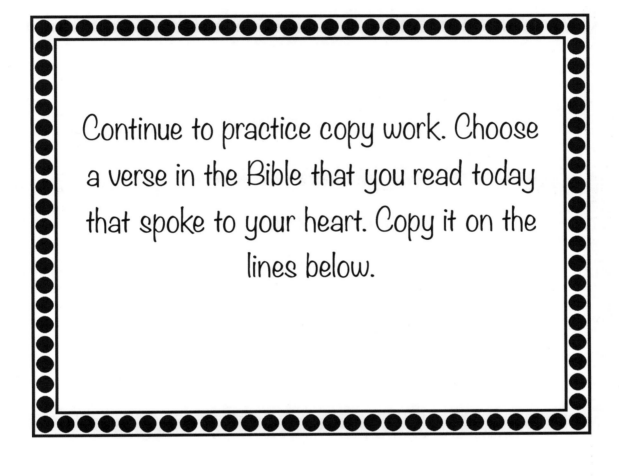

Continue to practice copy work. Choose a verse in the Bible that you read today that spoke to your heart. Copy it on the lines below.

_____

_____

_____

_____

_____

Reading and Language

Choose one of your classic novels to read.

(Read 5 pages)

Copy a paragraph from your book and circle all the nouns.

Remember a noun is a......person,place,thing, or idea !

Did you put a capital letter at the beginning of your sentences and punctuation at the end?

Historical Figure Book

(Read 5 to 10 pages)

Title:_____Author:_____

Did this person face any struggles during their life if so what were the struggles?

_____

_____

_____

_____

_____

How did they over come their struggles?

_____

_____

_____

_____

A Time In History

Ludwig Van Beethoven

Who was Beethoven?

Nature Study

Draw something in nature. Write one fact about your drawing.

_____

Math Time

Work in your math curriculum for 30 to 40 min.

Check when done. ___

Relax for a while and watch a tutorial or documentary for 30 min.

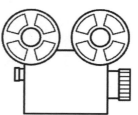 Movie Review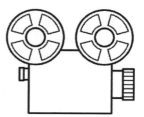

Write one thing you learned.

_____

Rate this movie. Color the stars.
5 stars mean it was Awesome!

Draw a scene from the movie.

Date :_____   Day 34

Bible Time

Read for 15 min. in your bible.

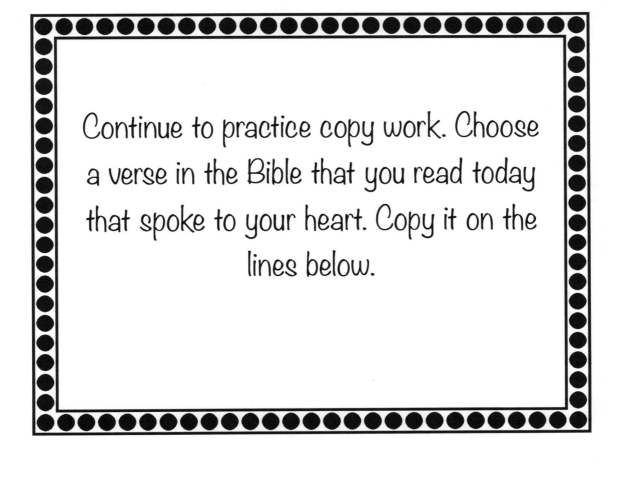

Continue to practice copy work. Choose a verse in the Bible that you read today that spoke to your heart. Copy it on the lines below.

_____

_____

_____

_____

_____

Reading and Language

Choose one of your classic novels to read.

(Read 5 pages)

Copy a paragraph from your book and circle all the verbs.

Remember a verb is an......action word !

_____

_____

_____

_____

_____

Did you put a capital letter at the beginning of your sentences and punctuation at the end?

Historical Figure Book

(Read 5 to 10 pages)

Title:_____ Author:_____

Tell about this persons education. Did they go to school? Draw a picture of what school might have looked like for them.

_____

_____

_____

_____

A Time In History

The Declaration of Independence

When was the Declaration of Independence signed?

_____

Nature Study

Draw something in nature. Write one fact about your drawing.

_____

Math Time

Work in your math curriculum for 30 to 40 min.

Check when done. ___

Relax for a while and watch a tutorial or documentary for 30 min.

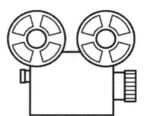
Movie Review
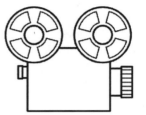

Write one thing you learned.

_____

Rate this movie. Color the stars.
5 stars mean it was Awesome!

Draw a scene from the movie.

Date :_____   Day 35

Bible Time

Read for 15 min. in your bible.

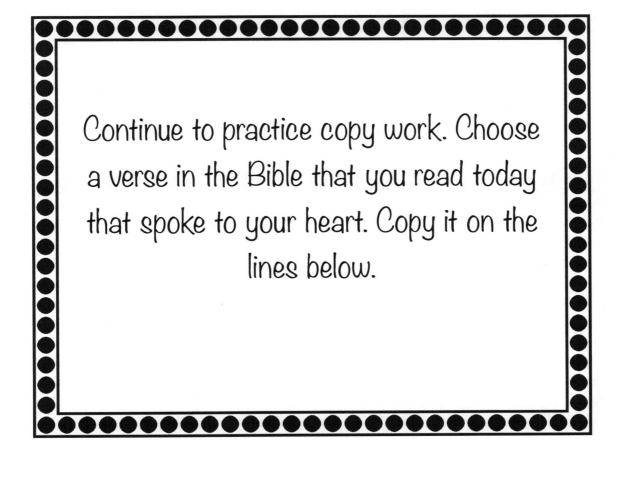

Continue to practice copy work. Choose a verse in the Bible that you read today that spoke to your heart. Copy it on the lines below.

_____

_____

_____

_____

_____

Reading and Language

Choose one of your classic novels to read.
(Read 5 pages)

Copy a paragraph from your book and circle all the adjectives.

Remember an adjective is a......describing word !

_____

_____

_____

_____

_____

Did you put a capital letter at the beginning of your sentences and punctuation at the end?

Historical Figure Book

(Read 5 to 10 pages)

Title:_____Author:_____

Draw a picture of a scene from your book.

A Time In History

De Soto Discovers the Mississippi

Nature Study

Draw something in nature. Write one fact about your drawing.

_____

Math Time

Work in your math curriculum for 30 to 40 min.

Check when done. ___

Relax for a while and watch a tutorial or documentary for 30 min.

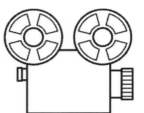 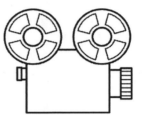

Movie Review

Write one thing you learned.

_____

Rate this movie. Color the stars.
5 stars mean it was Awesome!

Draw a scene from the movie.

Bible Time

Read for 15 min. in your bible.

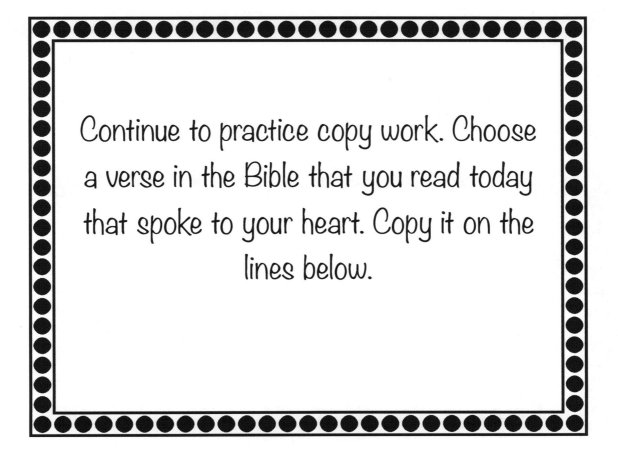

Continue to practice copy work. Choose a verse in the Bible that you read today that spoke to your heart. Copy it on the lines below.

_____

_____

_____

_____

Reading and Language

Choose one of your classic novels to read.
(Read 5 pages)
Copy a paragraph from your book and circle all the nouns.

Remember a noun is a......person, place, thing, or idea !

_____

_____

_____

_____

_____

Did you put a capital letter at the beginning of your
sentences and punctuation at the end?

Historical Figure Book

(Read 5 to 10 pages)

Title:_____Author:_____

If you could ask this person anything what would you ask?

_____

_____

Design a postage stamp in honor of this person.

A Time In History

Attila the Hun

Attila was a feared barbarian leader who led an army
and terrorized Asia and Europe.

Nature Study

Draw something in nature. Write one fact about your drawing.

_____

Math Time

Work in your math curriculum for 30 to 40 min.

Check when done. ___

Relax for a while and watch a tutorial or documentary for 30 min.

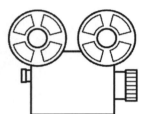

Movie Review

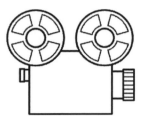

Write one thing you learned.

_____

Rate this movie. Color the stars.
5 stars mean it was Awesome!

Draw a scene from the movie.

Bible Time

Read for 15 min. in your bible.

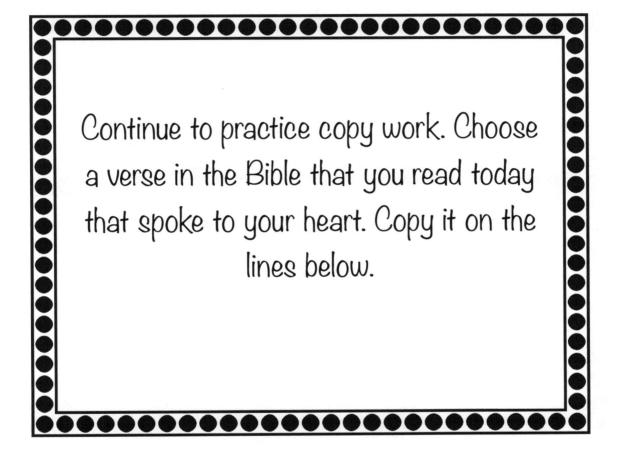

Continue to practice copy work. Choose a verse in the Bible that you read today that spoke to your heart. Copy it on the lines below.

_____

_____

_____

_____

Reading and Language

Choose one of your classic novels to read.
(Read 5 pages)

Copy a paragraph from your book and circle all the verbs.

Remember a verb is an......action word !

_____

_____

_____

_____

_____

Did you put a capital letter at the beginning of your
sentences and punctuation at the end?

Historical Figure Book

(Read 5 to 10 pages)

Title:_____Author:_____

Tell in your own words what you read.

_____

_____

_____

_____

_____

_____

_____

_____

_____

_____

A Time In History

Writer Jane Austen

Can you name a book that she wrote?

_____

Nature Study

Draw something in nature. Write one fact about your drawing.

_____

Math Time

Work in your math curriculum for 30 to 40 min.

Check when done. ___

Relax for a while and watch a tutorial or documentary for 30 min.

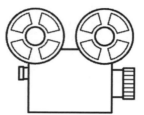 Movie Review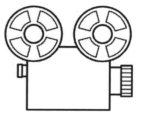

Write one thing you learned.

_____

Rate this movie. Color the stars.
5 stars mean it was Awesome!

Draw a scene from the movie.

Bible Time

Read for 15 min. in your bible.

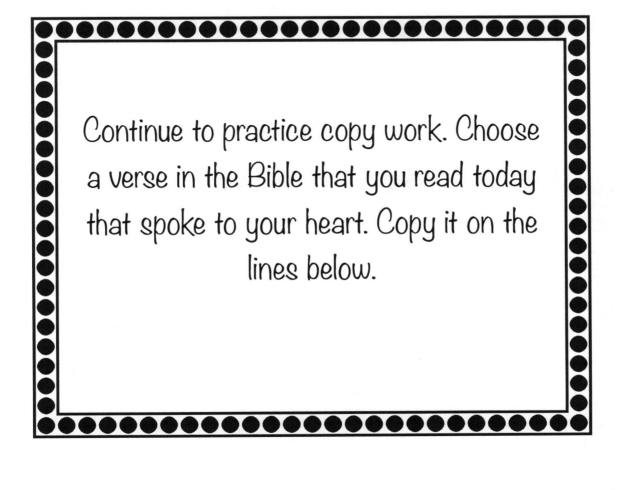

Continue to practice copy work. Choose a verse in the Bible that you read today that spoke to your heart. Copy it on the lines below.

_____

_____

_____

_____

Reading and Language

Choose one of your classic novels to read.

(Read 5 pages)

Copy a paragraph from your book and circle all the adjectives.

Remember an adjective is a......describing word !

_____

_____

_____

_____

_____

Did you put a capital letter at the beginning of your sentences and punctuation at the end?

Historical Figure Book

(Read 5 to 10 pages)

Title:_____Author:_____

How did this person die? Or if still alive what are they doing now?

_____

_____

_____

_____

_____

_____

_____

Draw a picture.

A Time In History

Edward Teach (Blackbeard)

He was an English pirate during 1717.

Nature Study

Draw something in nature. Write one fact about your drawing.

_____

Math Time

Work in your math curriculum for 30 to 40 min.

Check when done. ___

Relax for a while and watch a tutorial or documentary for 30 min.

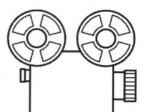

<u>Movie Review</u>

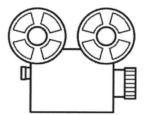

Write one thing you learned.

_____

Rate this movie. Color the stars.

5 stars mean it was Awesome!

Draw a scene from the movie.

Date : _____   Day 39

Bible Time

Read for 15 min. in your bible.

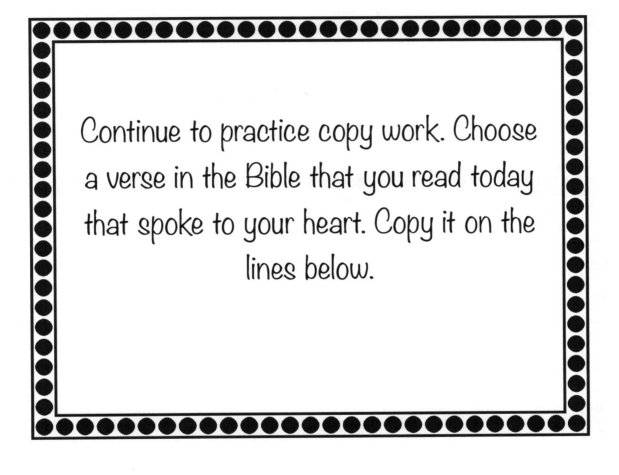

Continue to practice copy work. Choose a verse in the Bible that you read today that spoke to your heart. Copy it on the lines below.

_____

_____

_____

_____

Reading and Language

Choose one of your classic novels to read.

(Read 5 pages)

Copy a paragraph from your book and circle all the nouns.

Remember a noun is a......person,place,thing, or idea !

_____

_____

_____

_____

_____

Did you put a capital letter at the beginning of your
sentences and punctuation at the end?

Historical Figure Book

(Read 5 to 10 pages)

Title:_____Author:_____

Did you like learning about this person?
Tell why or why not.

_____

_____

_____

_____

_____

_____

_____

_____

_____

_____

A Time In History

Columbus Lands at San Salvador
October 14, 1492

Nature Study

Draw something in nature. Write one fact about your drawing.

_____

Math Time

Work in your math curriculum for 30 to 40 min.

Check when done. ___

Relax for a while and watch a tutorial or documentary for 30 min.

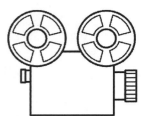 Movie Review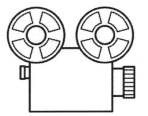

Write one thing you learned.

_____

Rate this movie. Color the stars.
5 stars mean it was Awesome!

Draw a scene from the movie.

Date : _____   Day 40

Bible Time

Read for 15 min. in your bible.

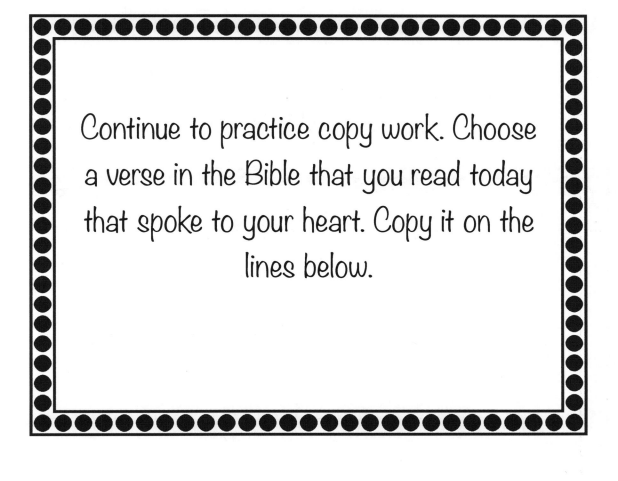

Continue to practice copy work. Choose
a verse in the Bible that you read today
that spoke to your heart. Copy it on the
lines below.

_____

_____

_____

_____

Reading and Language

Choose one of your classic novels to read.

(Read 5 pages)

Copy a paragraph from your book and circle all the verbs.

Remember a verb is an......action word !

_____

_____

_____

_____

_____

Did you put a capital letter at the beginning of your sentences and punctuation at the end?

Historical Figure Book

(Read 5 to 10 pages)

Title:_____Author:_____

Would you recommend this book to someone else?
Tell why you would recommend it.

_____

_____

_____

_____

_____

_____

_____

_____

_____

A Time In History

Mount Rushmore

What presidents faces are on Mt Rushmore?

_____

_____

_____

_____

Nature Study

Draw something in nature. Write one fact about your drawing.

_____

Math Time

Work in your math curriculum for 30 to 40 min.

Check when done. ___

Relax for a while and watch a tutorial or documentary for 30 min.

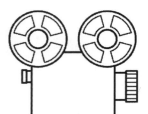 Movie Review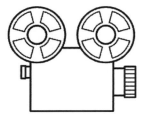

Write one thing you learned.

_____

Rate this movie. Color the stars.
5 stars mean it was Awesome!

Draw a scene from the movie.

Date :_____   Day 41

Bible Time

Read for 15 min. in your bible.

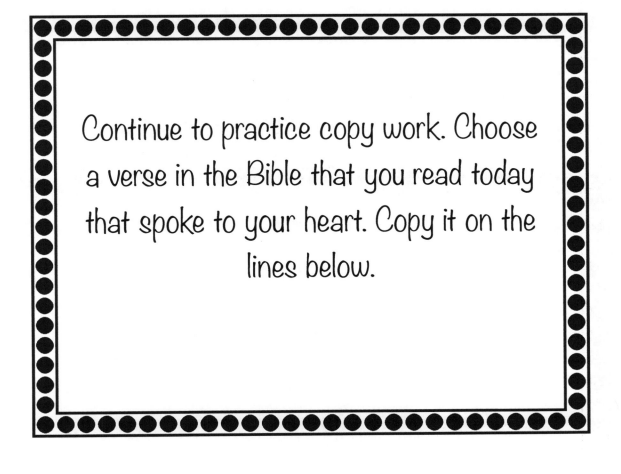

Continue to practice copy work. Choose a verse in the Bible that you read today that spoke to your heart. Copy it on the lines below.

_____

_____

_____

_____

Reading and Language

Choose one of your classic novels to read.

(Read 5 pages)

Copy a paragraph from your book and circle all the adjectives.

Remember an adjective is a.......describing word !

_____

_____

_____

_____

_____

_____

Did you put a capital letter at the beginning of your
sentences and punctuation at the end?

Historical Figure Book

(Read 5 to 10 pages)

Title:_____Author:_____

Who are you reading about?

_____

Where are they from?

_____

Color the map where this person lived or lives.

A Time In History

Statue of Liberty

From the ground to torch she stands at 305ft 1 inch.
The statue is located on Liberty Island Manhattan,
New York City, New York.

Nature Study

Draw something in nature. Write one fact about your drawing.

_____

Math Time

Work in your math curriculum for 30 to 40 min.

Check when done. ___

Relax for a while and watch a tutorial or documentary for 30 min.

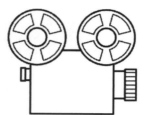 Movie Review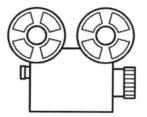

Write one thing you learned.

_____

Rate this movie. Color the stars.
5 stars mean it was Awesome!

Draw a scene from the movie.

Date :_____   Day 42

Bible Time

Read for 15 min. in your bible.

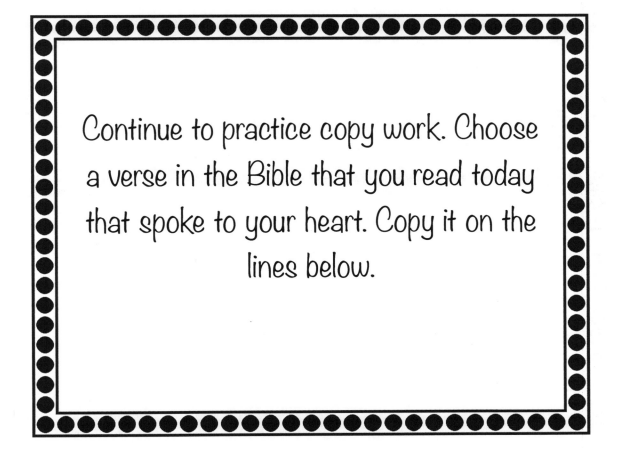

Continue to practice copy work. Choose a verse in the Bible that you read today that spoke to your heart. Copy it on the lines below.

_____

_____

_____

_____

Reading and Language

Choose one of your classic novels to read.
(Read 5 pages)
Copy a paragraph from your book and circle all the nouns.

Remember a noun is a......person,place,thing, or idea !

_____

_____

_____

_____

_____

Did you put a capital letter at the beginning of your
sentences and punctuation at the end?

Historical Figure Book

(Read 5 to 10 pages)

Title:_____Author:_____

Tell in your own words what you read today.

_____

_____

_____

_____

_____

_____

_____

When did this person live or if still alive, when was this person born?

_____

A Time In History

Aztec Calendar

The Aztec stone was carved from solidified lava in the late 15th century.

Nature Study

Draw something in nature. Write one fact about your drawing.

_____

Math Time

Work in your math curriculum for 30 to 40 min.

Check when done. ___

Relax for a while and watch a tutorial or documentary for 30 min.

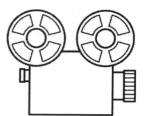 Movie Review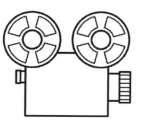

Write one thing you learned.

_____

Rate this movie. Color the stars.
5 stars mean it was Awesome!

Draw a scene from the movie.

Date : _____   Day 43

Bible Time

Read for 15 min. in your bible.

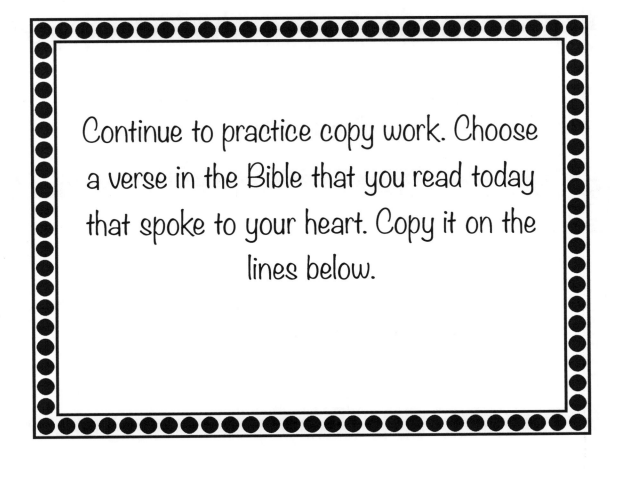

Continue to practice copy work. Choose a verse in the Bible that you read today that spoke to your heart. Copy it on the lines below.

_____

_____

_____

_____

Reading and Language

Choose one of your classic novels to read.

(Read 5 pages)

Copy a paragraph from your book and circle all the verbs.

Remember a verb is an......action word !

Did you put a capital letter at the beginning of your sentences and punctuation at the end?

Historical Figure Book

(Read 5 to 10 pages)

Title:_____Author:_____

Draw a portrait of your historical figure.

A Time In History

After looking at pictures and learning about different people , places and things in history lets learn about dates in history.

Write Todays Date

_____

Look up what important thing happened in history on this day?

_____

_____

_____

Draw a picture of what happened.

Nature Study

Draw something in nature. Write one fact about your drawing.

_____

Math Time

Work in your math curriculum for 30 to 40 min.

Check when done. ___

Relax for a while and watch a tutorial or documentary for 30 min.

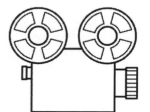 Movie Review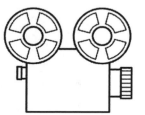

Write one thing you learned.

_____

Rate this movie. Color the stars.
5 stars mean it was Awesome!

Draw a scene from the movie.

Date : _____   Day 44

Bible Time

Read for 15 min. in your bible.

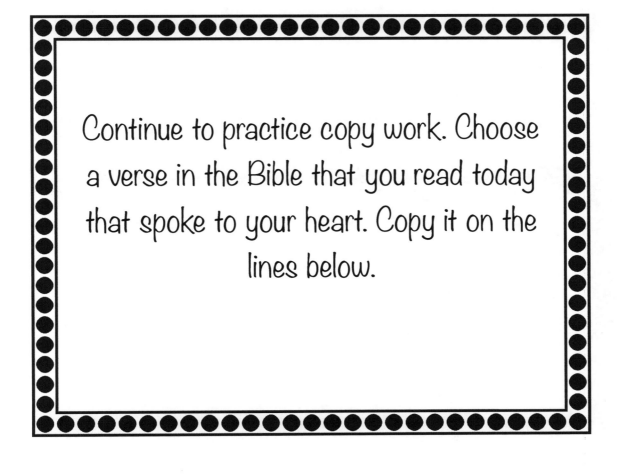

Continue to practice copy work. Choose
a verse in the Bible that you read today
that spoke to your heart. Copy it on the
lines below.

_____

_____

_____

_____

_____

Reading and Language

Choose one of your classic novels to read.
(Read 5 pages)
Copy a paragraph from your book and circle all the adjectives.

Remember an adjective is a......describing word !

_____

_____

_____

_____

_____

Did you put a capital letter at the beginning of your sentences and punctuation at the end?

Historical Figure Book

(Read 5 to 10 pages)

Title:_____Author:_____

Where does your story take place? Describe what the place looks like then draw a picture.

_____

_____

_____

_____

_____

A Time In History

After looking at pictures and learning about different people , places and things in history lets learn about dates in history.

Write Todays Date

_____

Look up what important thing happened in history on this day?

_____

_____

_____

Draw a picture of what happened.

Nature Study

Draw something in nature. Write one fact about your drawing.

_____

Math Time

Work in your math curriculum for 30 to 40 min.

Check when done. ___

Relax for a while and watch a tutorial or documentary for 30 min.

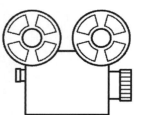 Movie Review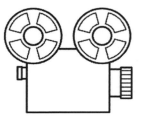

Write one thing you learned.

_____

Rate this movie. Color the stars.
5 stars mean it was Awesome!

Draw a scene from the movie.

Date :_____   Day 45

Bible Time

Read for 15 min. in your bible.

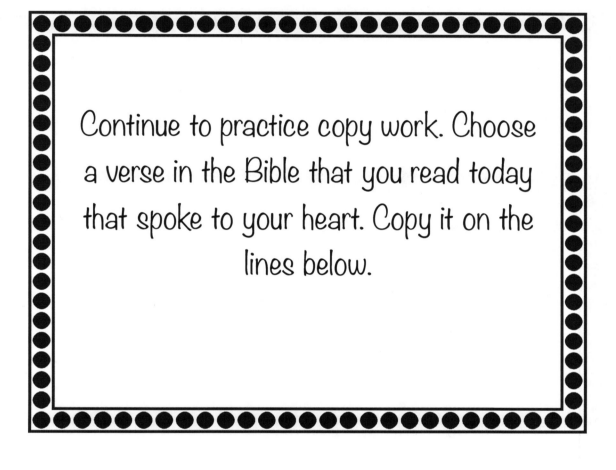

Continue to practice copy work. Choose a verse in the Bible that you read today that spoke to your heart. Copy it on the lines below.

_____

_____

_____

_____

Reading and Language

Choose one of your classic novels to read.
(Read 5 pages)
Copy a paragraph from your book and circle all the nouns.

Remember a noun is a......person,place,thing, or idea !

_____

_____

_____

_____

_____

Did you put a capital letter at the beginning of your
sentences and punctuation at the end?

Historical Figure Book

(Read 5 to 10 pages)

Title:_____ Author:_____

What is this person famous for? Draw a picture of
what they are famous for.

_____

_____

A Time In History

After looking at pictures and learning about different people , places and things in history lets learn about dates in history.

Write Todays Date

_____

Look up what important thing happened in history on this day?

_____

_____

_____

Draw a picture of what happened.

Nature Study

Draw something in nature. Write one fact about your drawing.

_____

Math Time

Work in your math curriculum for 30 to 40 min.

Check when done. ___

Relax for a while and watch a tutorial or documentary for 30 min.

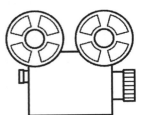 ## Movie Review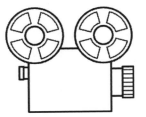

Write one thing you learned.

_____

Rate this movie. Color the stars.
5 stars mean it was Awesome!

Draw a scene from the movie.

Bible Time

Read for 15 min. in your bible.

Continue to practice copy work. Choose a verse in the Bible that you read today that spoke to your heart. Copy it on the lines below.

_____

_____

_____

_____

Reading and Language

Choose one of your classic novels to read.
(Read 5 pages)
Copy a paragraph from your book and circle all the verbs.

Remember a verb is an......action word !

_____

_____

_____

_____

_____

Did you put a capital letter at the beginning of your sentences and punctuation at the end?

Historical Figure Book

(Read 5 to 10 pages)

Title:_____Author:_____

What is the most interesting thing you learned?

_____

_____

_____

List four words to describe this person.

_____

_____

_____

_____

A Time In History

After looking at pictures and learning about different people , places and things in history lets learn about dates in history.

Write Todays Date

_____

Look up what important thing happened in history on this day?

_____

_____

_____

Draw a picture of what happened.

Nature Study

Draw something in nature. Write one fact about your drawing.

_____

Math Time

Work in your math curriculum for 30 to 40 min.

Check when done. ___

Relax for a while and watch a tutorial or documentary for 30 min.

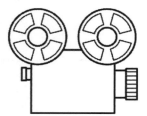 Movie Review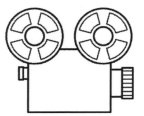

Write one thing you learned.

_____

Rate this movie. Color the stars.
5 stars mean it was Awesome!

Draw a scene from the movie.

Date :_____   Day 47

Bible Time

Read for 15 min. in your bible.

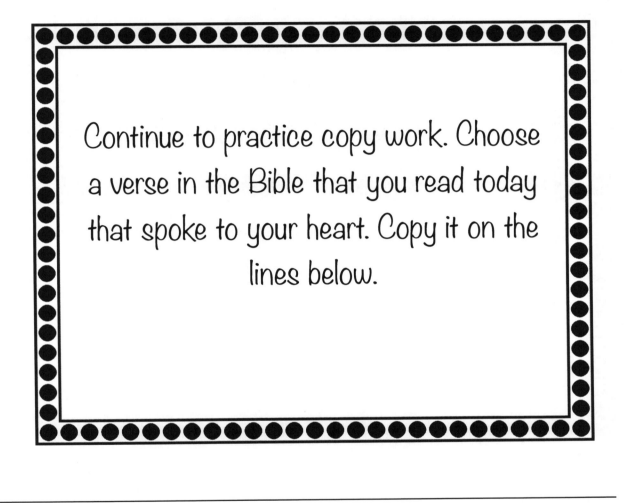

Continue to practice copy work. Choose a verse in the Bible that you read today that spoke to your heart. Copy it on the lines below.

_____

_____

_____

_____

Reading and Language

Choose one of your classic novels to read.

(Read 5 pages)

Copy a paragraph from your book and circle all the adjectives.

Remember an adjective is a......describing word !

_____

_____

_____

_____

_____

Did you put a capital letter at the beginning of your sentences and punctuation at the end?

Historical Figure Book
(Read 5 to 10 pages)

Title:_____Author:_____

Tell in your own words what you read.

_____

_____

_____

_____

_____

_____

_____

_____

_____

A Time In History

After looking at pictures and learning about different people , places and things in history lets learn about dates in history.

Write Todays Date

_____

Look up what important thing happened in history on this day?

_____

_____

_____

Draw a picture of what happened.

Nature Study

Draw something in nature. Write one fact about your drawing.

_____

Math Time

Work in your math curriculum for 30 to 40 min.

Check when done. ___

Relax for a while and watch a tutorial or documentary for 30 min.

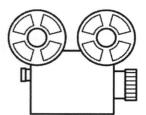 Movie Review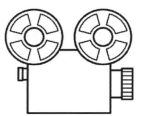

Write one thing you learned.

_____

Rate this movie. Color the stars.
5 stars mean it was Awesome!

Draw a scene from the movie.

Bible Time

Read for 15 min. in your bible.

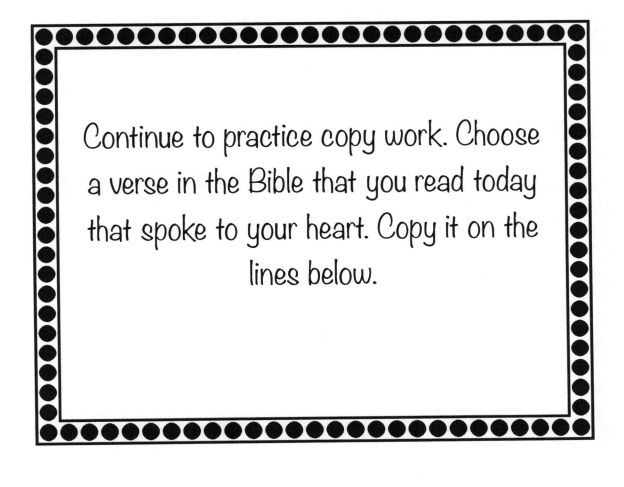

Continue to practice copy work. Choose a verse in the Bible that you read today that spoke to your heart. Copy it on the lines below.

_____

_____

_____

_____

_____

Reading and Language

Choose one of your classic novels to read.

(Read 5 pages)

Copy a paragraph from your book and circle all the nouns.

Remember a noun is a......person,place,thing, or idea !

_____

_____

_____

_____

_____

Did you put a capital letter at the beginning of your sentences and punctuation at the end?

Historical Figure Book

(Read 5 to 10 pages)

Title:_____Author:_____

Tell in your own words what you read.

_____

_____

_____

_____

_____

_____

_____

_____

_____

_____

A Time In History

After looking at pictures and learning about different people , places and things in history lets learn about dates in history.

Write Todays Date

_____

Look up what important thing happened in history on this day?

_____

_____

_____

Draw a picture of what happened.

Nature Study

Draw something in nature. Write one fact about your drawing.

_____

Math Time

Work in your math curriculum for 30 to 40 min.

Check when done. ___

Relax for a while and watch a tutorial or documentary for 30 min.

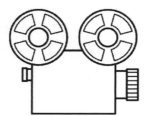 Movie Review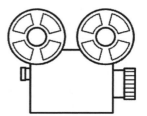

Write one thing you learned.

_____

Rate this movie. Color the stars.
5 stars mean it was Awesome!

Draw a scene from the movie.

Date : _____

Day 49

Bible Time

Read for 15 min. in your bible.

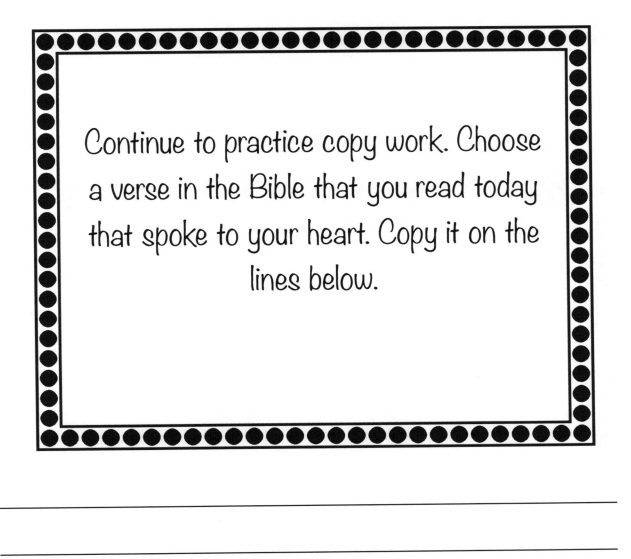

Continue to practice copy work. Choose a verse in the Bible that you read today that spoke to your heart. Copy it on the lines below.

_____

_____

_____

_____

_____

Reading and Language

Choose one of your classic novels to read.
(Read 5 pages)
Copy a paragraph from your book and circle all the verbs.

Remember a verb is an......action word !

_____

_____

_____

_____

_____

Did you put a capital letter at the beginning of your
sentences and punctuation at the end?

Historical Figure Book

(Read 5 to 10 pages)

Title:_____Author:_____

Tell me about this persons character.

_____

_____

_____

Do you think this is a person you would like to be friends with?

_____

_____

_____

_____

_____

_____

A Time In History

After looking at pictures and learning about different people , places and things in history lets learn about dates in history.

Write Todays Date

_____

Look up what important thing happened in history on this day?

_____

_____

_____

Draw a picture of what happened.

Nature Study

Draw something in nature. Write one fact about your drawing.

_____

Math Time

Work in your math curriculum for 30 to 40 min.

Check when done. ___

Relax for a while and watch a tutorial or documentary for 30 min.

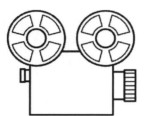 Movie Review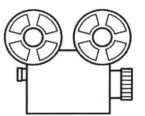

Write one thing you learned.

_____

Rate this movie. Color the stars.
5 stars mean it was Awesome!

Draw a scene from the movie.

Date :_____   Day 50

Bible Time

Read for 15 min. in your bible.

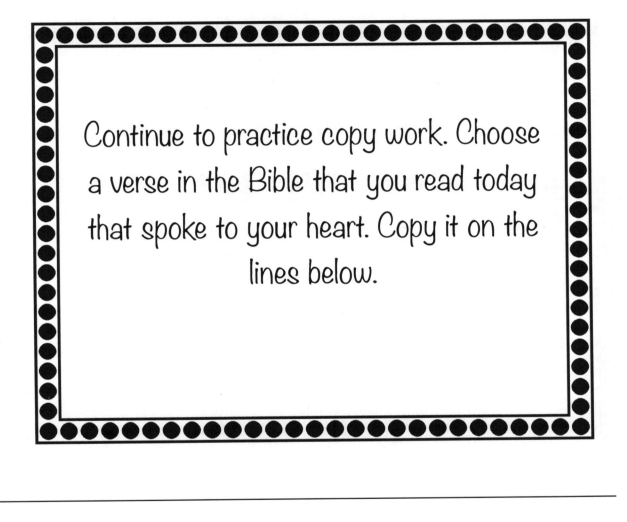

Continue to practice copy work. Choose a verse in the Bible that you read today that spoke to your heart. Copy it on the lines below.

_____

_____

_____

_____

_____

Reading and Language

Choose one of your classic novels to read.

(Read 5 pages)

Copy a paragraph from your book and circle all the adjectives.

Remember an adjective is a.....describing word !

_____

_____

_____

_____

_____

Did you put a capital letter at the beginning of your sentences and punctuation at the end?

Historical Figure Book

(Read 5 to 10 pages)

Title:_____Author:_____

Do you think you could live during the time of your historical figure? Tell why or why not.

_____

_____

_____

_____

_____

_____

_____

_____

_____

_____

A Time In History

After looking at pictures and learning about different people , places and things in history lets learn about dates in history.

Write Todays Date

_____

Look up what important thing happened in history on this day?

_____

_____

_____

Draw a picture of what happened.

Nature Study

Draw something in nature. Write one fact about your drawing.

_____

Math Time

Work in your math curriculum for 30 to 40 min.

Check when done. ___

Relax for a while and watch a tutorial or documentary for 30 min.

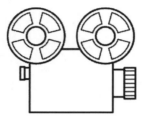 Movie Review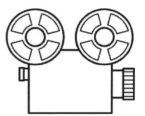

Write one thing you learned.

_____

Rate this movie. Color the stars.
5 stars mean it was Awesome!

Draw a scene from the movie.

Date :_____   Day 51

Bible Time

Read for 15 min. in your bible.

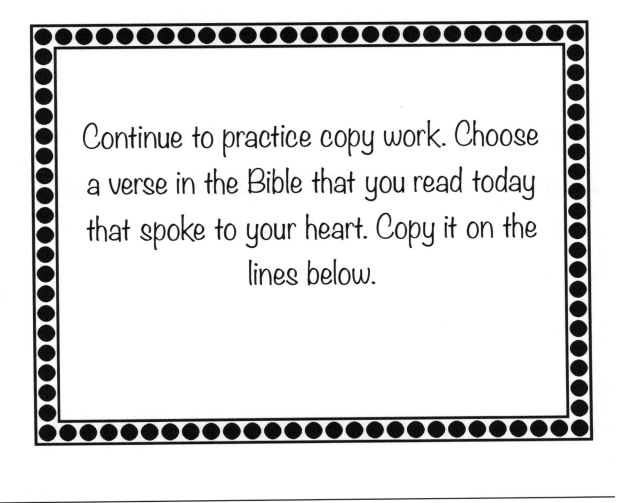

Continue to practice copy work. Choose a verse in the Bible that you read today that spoke to your heart. Copy it on the lines below.

_____

_____

_____

_____

Reading and Language

Choose one of your classic novels to read.

(Read 5 pages)

Copy a paragraph from your book and circle all the nouns.

Remember a noun is a......person, place, thing, or idea !

_____

_____

_____

_____

_____

_____

Did you put a capital letter at the beginning of your sentences and punctuation at the end?

Historical Figure Book

(Read 5 to 10 pages)

Title:_____ Author:_____

What era is this person from?

Draw the type of clothing they wore or wear.

_____

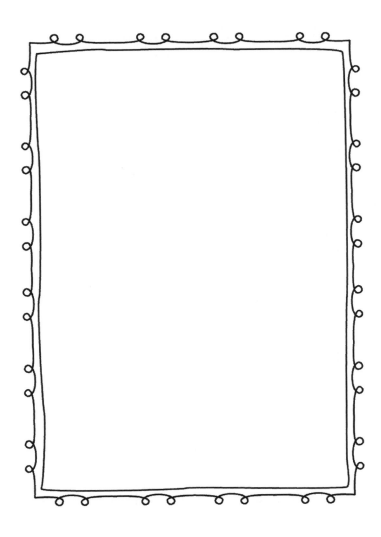

A Time In History

After looking at pictures and learning about different people , places and things in history lets learn about dates in history.

Write Todays Date

_____

Look up what important thing happened in history on this day?

_____

_____

_____

Draw a picture of what happened.

Nature Study

Draw something in nature. Write one fact about your drawing.

_____

Math Time

Work in your math curriculum for 30 to 40 min.

Check when done. ___

Relax for a while and watch a tutorial or documentary for 30 min.

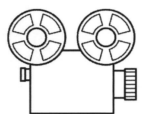 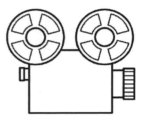

Movie Review

Write one thing you learned.

_____

Rate this movie. Color the stars.
5 stars mean it was Awesome!

Draw a scene from the movie.

Date : _____   Day 52

Bible Time

Read for 15 min. in your bible.

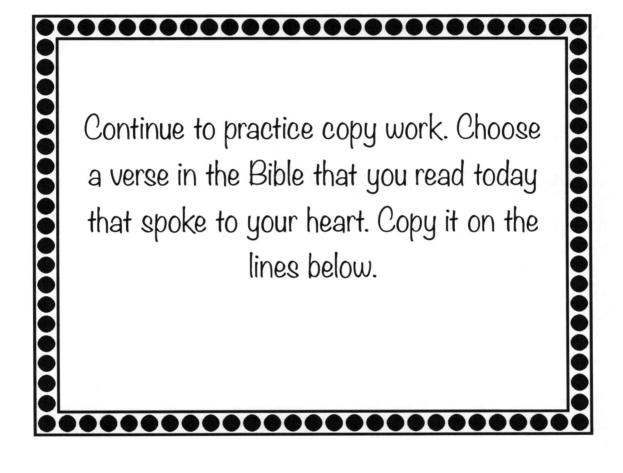

Continue to practice copy work. Choose a verse in the Bible that you read today that spoke to your heart. Copy it on the lines below.

_____

_____

_____

_____

_____

Reading and Language

Choose one of your classic novels to read.

(Read 5 pages)

Copy a paragraph from your book and circle all the verbs.

Remember a verb is an......action word !

_____

_____

_____

_____

_____

Did you put a capital letter at the beginning of your sentences and punctuation at the end?

Historical Figure Book

(Read 5 to 10 pages)

Title:_____Author:_____

Tell in your own words what you read today.

_____

_____

_____

_____

_____

_____

_____

_____

_____

A Time In History

After looking at pictures and learning about different people , places and things in history lets learn about dates in history.

Write Todays Date

_____

Look up what important thing happened in history on this day?

_____

_____

_____

Draw a picture of what happened.

Nature Study

Draw something in nature. Write one fact about your drawing.

_____

Math Time

Work in your math curriculum for 30 to 40 min.

Check when done. ___

Relax for a while and watch a tutorial or documentary for 30 min.

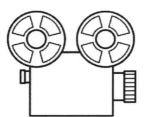 <u>Movie Review</u>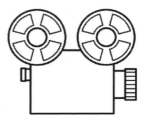

Write one thing you learned.

_____

Rate this movie. Color the stars.
5 stars mean it was Awesome!

Draw a scene from the movie.

Bible Time

Read for 15 min. in your bible.

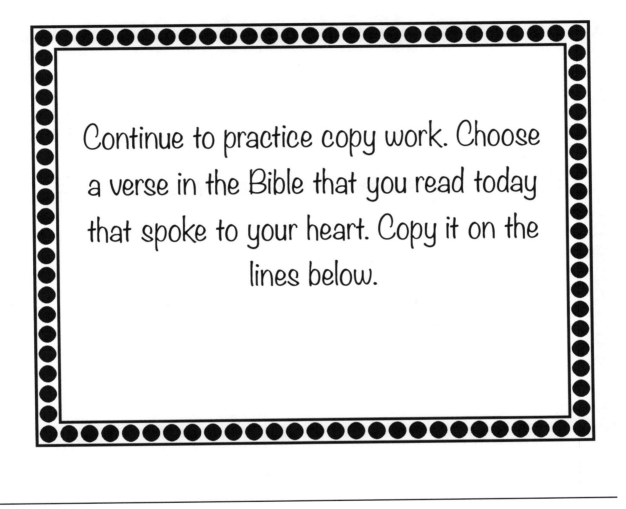

Continue to practice copy work. Choose a verse in the Bible that you read today that spoke to your heart. Copy it on the lines below.

Reading and Language

Choose one of your classic novels to read.

(Read 5 pages)

Copy a paragraph from your book and circle all the adjectives.

Remember an adjective is a.....describing word !

_____

_____

_____

_____

_____

Did you put a capital letter at the beginning of your sentences and punctuation at the end?

Historical Figure Book

(Read 5 to 10 pages)

Title:_____Author:_____

Did this person face any struggles during their life if so what were the struggles?

_____

_____

_____

_____

_____

How did they over come their struggles?

_____

_____

_____

_____

A Time In History

After looking at pictures and learning about different people , places and things in history lets learn about dates in history.

Write Todays Date

_____

Look up what important thing happened in history on this day?

_____

_____

_____

Draw a picture of what happened.

Nature Study

Draw something in nature. Write one fact about your drawing.

_____

Math Time

Work in your math curriculum for 30 to 40 min.

Check when done. ___

Relax for a while and watch a tutorial or documentary for 30 min.

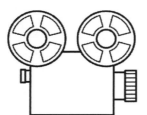 Movie Review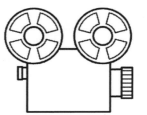

Write one thing you learned.

_____

Rate this movie. Color the stars.
5 stars mean it was Awesome!

Draw a scene from the movie.

Date :_____

Bible Time

Read for 15 min. in your bible.

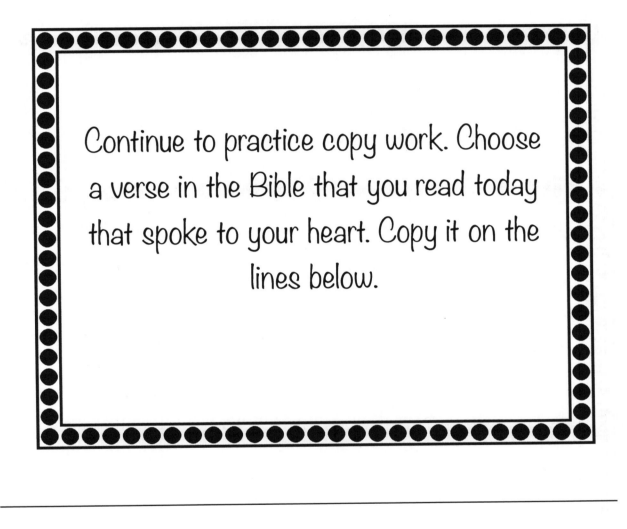

Continue to practice copy work. Choose a verse in the Bible that you read today that spoke to your heart. Copy it on the lines below.

_____

_____

_____

_____

_____

Reading and Language

Choose one of your classic novels to read.

(Read 5 pages)

Copy a paragraph from your book and circle all the nouns.

Remember a noun is a......person,place,thing, or idea !

_____

_____

_____

_____

_____

Did you put a capital letter at the beginning of your
sentences and punctuation at the end?

Historical Figure Book

(Read 5 to 10 pages)

Title:_____Author:_____

Tell about this persons education. Did they go to school? Draw a picture of what school might have looked like for them.

_____

_____

_____

_____

A Time In History

After looking at pictures and learning about different people , places and things in history lets learn about dates in history.

Write Todays Date

_____

Look up what important thing happened in history on this day?

_____

_____

_____

Draw a picture of what happened.

Nature Study

Draw something in nature. Write one fact about your drawing.

_____

Math Time

Work in your math curriculum for 30 to 40 min.

Check when done. ___

Relax for a while and watch a tutorial or documentary for 30 min.

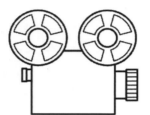 Movie Review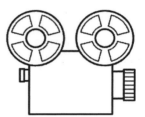

Write one thing you learned.

_____

Rate this movie. Color the stars.
5 stars mean it was Awesome!

Draw a scene from the movie.

Date :_____

Bible Time

Read for 15 min. in your bible.

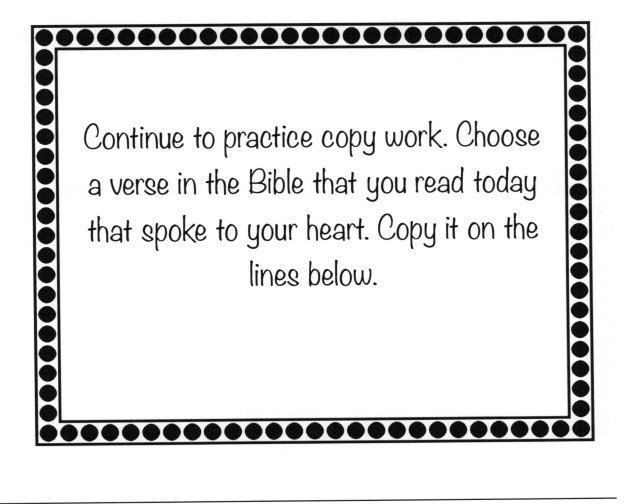

Continue to practice copy work. Choose a verse in the Bible that you read today that spoke to your heart. Copy it on the lines below.

_____

_____

_____

_____

_____

Reading and Language

Choose one of your classic novels to read.

(Read 5 pages)

Copy a paragraph from your book and circle all the verbs.

Remember a verb is an......action word !

Did you put a capital letter at the beginning of your sentences and punctuation at the end?

Historical Figure Book

(Read 5 to 10 pages)

Title:_____Author:_____

Draw a picture of a scene from your book.

A Time In History

After looking at pictures and learning about different people , places and things in history lets learn about dates in history.

Write Todays Date

_____

Look up what important thing happened in history on this day?

_____

_____

_____

Draw a picture of what happened.

Nature Study

Draw something in nature. Write one fact about your drawing.

_____

Math Time

Work in your math curriculum for 30 to 40 min.

Check when done. ___

Relax for a while and watch a tutorial or documentary for 30 min.

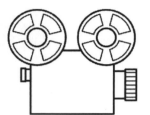 Movie Review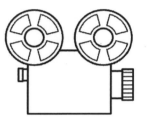

Write one thing you learned.

_____

Rate this movie. Color the stars.
5 stars mean it was Awesome!

Draw a scene from the movie.

Date :_____   Day 56

Bible Time

Read for 15 min. in your bible.

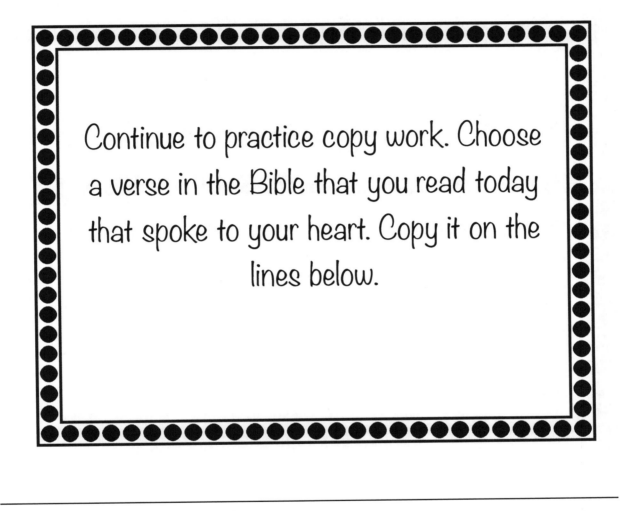

Continue to practice copy work. Choose a verse in the Bible that you read today that spoke to your heart. Copy it on the lines below.

_____

_____

_____

_____

Reading and Language

Choose one of your classic novels to read.
(Read 5 pages)
Copy a paragraph from your book and circle all the adjectives.

Remember an adjective is a......describing word !

_____

_____

_____

_____

_____

Did you put a capital letter at the beginning of your
sentences and punctuation at the end?

Historical Figure Book

(Read 5 to 10 pages)

Title:_____Author:_____

If you could ask this person anything what would you ask?

_____

_____

Design a postage stamp in honor of this person.

A Time In History

After looking at pictures and learning about different people , places and things in history lets learn about dates in history.

Write Todays Date

_____

Look up what important thing happened in history on this day?

_____

_____

_____

Draw a picture of what happened.

Nature Study

Draw something in nature. Write one fact about your drawing.

_____

Math Time

Work in your math curriculum for 30 to 40 min.

Check when done. ___

Relax for a while and watch a tutorial or documentary for 30 min.

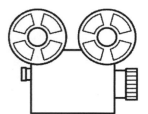 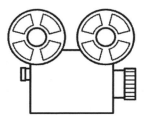

Movie Review

Write one thing you learned.

_____

Rate this movie. Color the stars.
5 stars mean it was Awesome!

Draw a scene from the movie.

Date : _____   Day 57

Bible Time

Read for 15 min. in your bible.

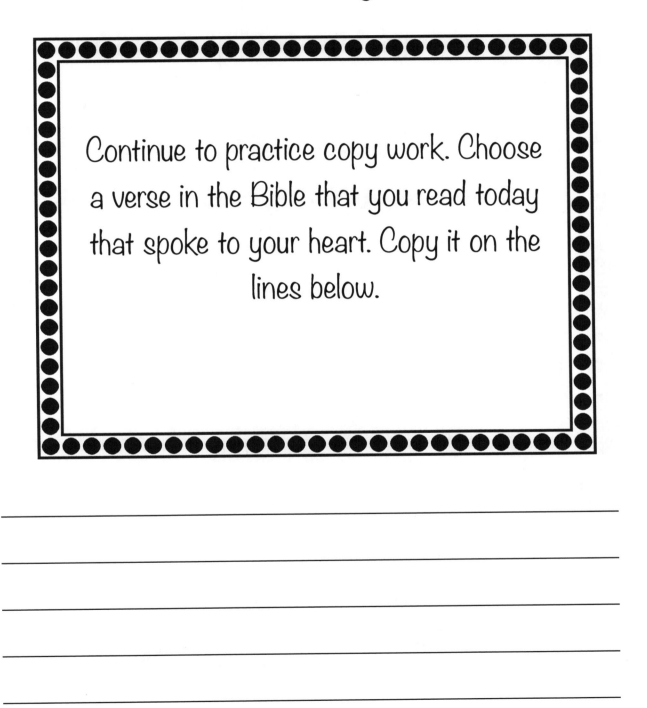

Continue to practice copy work. Choose a verse in the Bible that you read today that spoke to your heart. Copy it on the lines below.

_____

_____

_____

_____

Reading and Language

Choose one of your classic novels to read.
(Read 5 pages)
Copy a paragraph from your book and circle all the nouns.

Remember a noun is a......person,place,thing, or idea !

_____

_____

_____

_____

_____

Did you put a capital letter at the beginning of your
sentences and punctuation at the end?

Historical Figure Book

(Read 5 to 10 pages)

Title:_____Author:_____

Tell in your own words what you read today.

_____

_____

_____

_____

_____

_____

_____

_____

A Time In History

After looking at pictures and learning about different people , places and things in history lets learn about dates in history.

Write Todays Date

_____

Look up what important thing happened in history on this day?

_____

_____

_____

Draw a picture of what happened.

Nature Study

Draw something in nature. Write one fact about your drawing.

_____

Math Time

Work in your math curriculum for 30 to 40 min.

Check when done. ___

Relax for a while and watch a tutorial or documentary for 30 min.

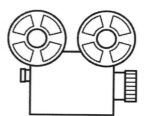

Movie Review

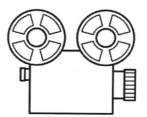

Write one thing you learned.

_____

Rate this movie. Color the stars.
5 stars mean it was Awesome!

Draw a scene from the movie.

Date :_____

Bible Time

Read for 15 min. in your bible.

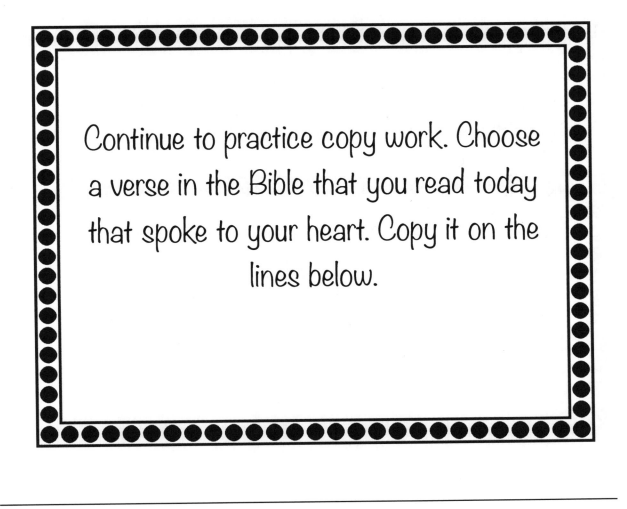

Continue to practice copy work. Choose a verse in the Bible that you read today that spoke to your heart. Copy it on the lines below.

_____

_____

_____

_____

Reading and Language

Choose one of your classic novels to read.

(Read 5 pages)

Copy a paragraph from your book and circle all the verbs.

Remember a verb is an......action word !

_____

_____

_____

_____

_____

Did you put a capital letter at the beginning of your sentences and punctuation at the end?

Historical Figure Book

(Read 5 to 10 pages)

Title:_____Author:_____

How did this person die? Or if still alive what are they doing now?

_____

_____

_____

_____

_____

_____

_____

Draw a picture.

A Time In History

After looking at pictures and learning about different people , places and things in history lets learn about dates in history.

Write Todays Date

_____

Look up what important thing happened in history on this day?

_____

_____

_____

Draw a picture of what happened.

Nature Study

Draw something in nature. Write one fact about your drawing.

_____

Math Time

Work in your math curriculum for 30 to 40 min.

Check when done. ___

Relax for a while and watch a tutorial or documentary for 30 min.

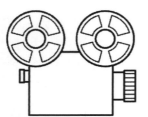 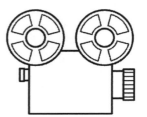

Movie Review

Write one thing you learned.

_____

Rate this movie. Color the stars.
5 stars mean it was Awesome!

Draw a scene from the movie.

Date :_____

Bible Time

Read for 15 min. in your bible.

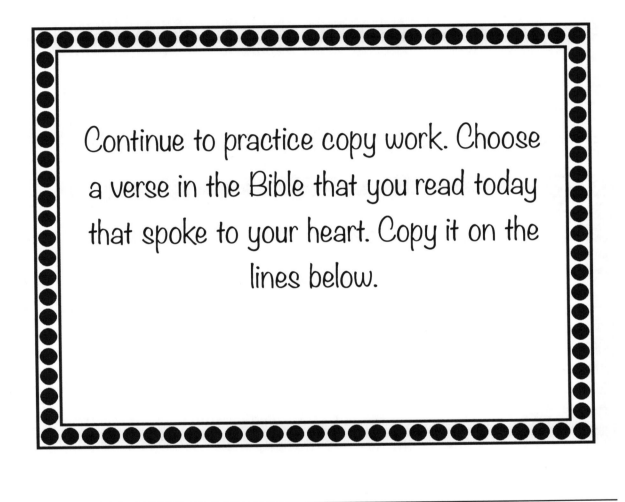

Continue to practice copy work. Choose a verse in the Bible that you read today that spoke to your heart. Copy it on the lines below.

_____

_____

_____

_____

Reading and Language

Choose one of your classic novels to read.
(Read 5 pages)

Copy a paragraph from your book and circle all the adjectives.

Remember an adjective is a.....describing word !

_____

_____

_____

_____

_____

Did you put a capital letter at the beginning of your sentences and punctuation at the end?

Historical Figure Book

(Read 5 to 10 pages)

Title:_____Author:_____

Did you like learning about this person?
Tell why or why not.

_____

_____

_____

_____

_____

_____

_____

_____

_____

A Time In History

After looking at pictures and learning about different people , places and things in history lets learn about dates in history.

Write Todays Date

_____

Look up what important thing happened in history on this day?

_____

_____

_____

Draw a picture of what happened.

Nature Study

Draw something in nature. Write one fact about your drawing.

_____

Math Time

Work in your math curriculum for 30 to 40 min.

Check when done. ___

Relax for a while and watch a tutorial or documentary for 30 min.

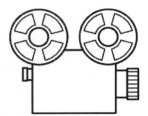

<u>Movie Review</u>

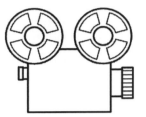

Write one thing you learned.

_____

Rate this movie. Color the stars.
5 stars mean it was Awesome!

Draw a scene from the movie.

Date : _____   Day 60

Bible Time

Read for 15 min. in your bible.

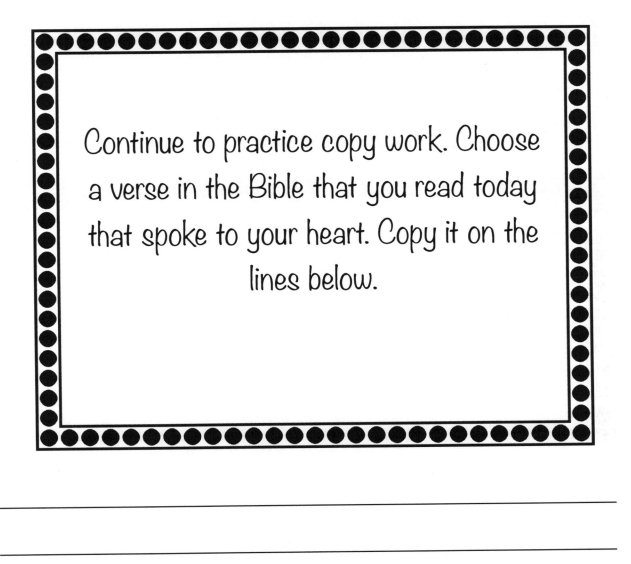

Continue to practice copy work. Choose a verse in the Bible that you read today that spoke to your heart. Copy it on the lines below.

_____

_____

_____

_____

_____

Reading and Language

Choose one of your classic novels to read.

(Read 5 pages)

Copy a paragraph from your book and circle all the nouns.

Remember a noun is a......person,place,thing, or idea !

_____

_____

_____

_____

_____

Did you put a capital letter at the beginning of your sentences and punctuation at the end?

Historical Figure Book

(Read 5 to 10 pages)

Title:_____Author:_____

Would you recommend this book to someone else?
Tell why you would recommend it.

_____

_____

_____

_____

_____

_____

_____

_____

A Time In History

After looking at pictures and learning about different people , places and things in history lets learn about dates in history.

Write Todays Date

_____

Look up what important thing happened in history on this day?

_____

_____

_____

Draw a picture of what happened.

Nature Study

Draw something in nature. Write one fact about your drawing.

_____

Math Time

Work in your math curriculum for 30 to 40 min.

Check when done. ___

Relax for a while and watch a tutorial or documentary for 30 min.

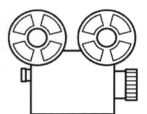 ### Movie Review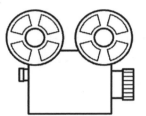

Write one thing you learned.

_____

Rate this movie. Color the stars.
5 stars mean it was Awesome!

Draw a scene from the movie.

Date : _____

Bible Time

Read for 15 min. in your bible.

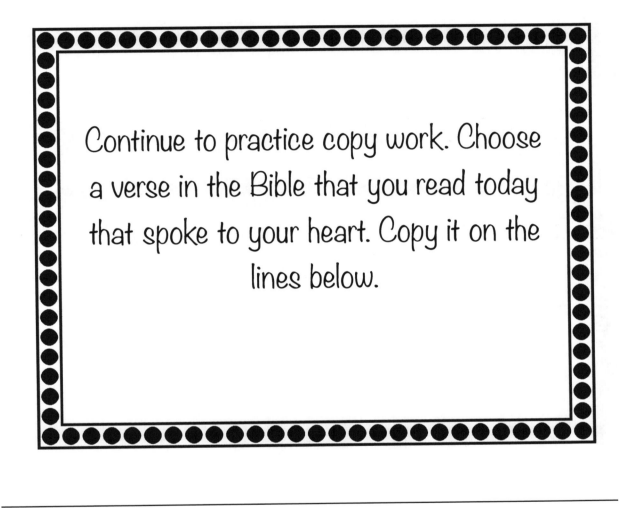

Continue to practice copy work. Choose a verse in the Bible that you read today that spoke to your heart. Copy it on the lines below.

_____

_____

_____

_____

_____

Reading and Language

Choose one of your classic novels to read.

(Read 5 pages)

Copy a paragraph from your book and circle all the verbs.

Remember a verb is an......action word !

_____

_____

_____

_____

_____

Did you put a capital letter at the beginning of your sentences and punctuation at the end?

Historical Figure Book

(Read 5 to 10 pages)

Title:_____Author:_____

Who are you reading about?

_____

Where are they from?

_____

Color the map where this person lived or lives.A Time In History

A Time In History

After looking at pictures and learning about different people , places and things in history lets learn about dates in history.

Write Todays Date

_____

Look up what important thing happened in history on this day?

_____

_____

_____

Draw a picture of what happened.

Nature Study

Draw something in nature. Write one fact about your drawing.

_____

Math Time

Work in your math curriculum for 30 to 40 min.

Check when done. ___

Relax for a while and watch a tutorial or documentary for 30 min.

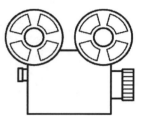 <u>Movie Review</u>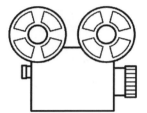

Write one thing you learned.

_____

Rate this movie. Color the stars.
5 stars mean it was Awesome!

Draw a scene from the movie.

Date :_____   Day 62

Bible Time

Read for 15 min. in your bible.

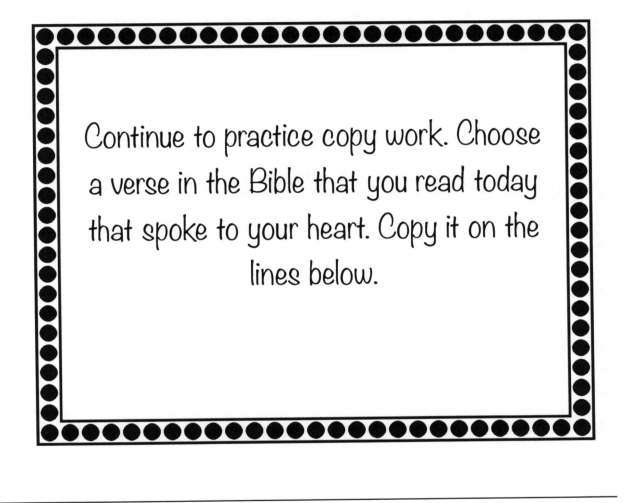

Continue to practice copy work. Choose a verse in the Bible that you read today that spoke to your heart. Copy it on the lines below.

_____

_____

_____

_____

_____

Reading and Language

Choose one of your classic novels to read.
(Read 5 pages)

Copy a paragraph from your book and circle all the adjectives.

Remember an adjective is a.....describing word !

_____

_____

_____

_____

_____

Did you put a capital letter at the beginning of your
sentences and punctuation at the end?

Historical Figure Book

(Read 5 to 10 pages)

Title:_____Author:_____

Tell in your own words what you read today.

_____

_____

_____

_____

_____

_____

_____

When did this person live or if still alive, when was this person born?

_____

A Time In History

After looking at pictures and learning about different people , places and things in history lets learn about dates in history.

Write Todays Date

_____

Look up what important thing happened in history on this day?

_____

_____

_____

Draw a picture of what happened.

Nature Study

Draw something in nature. Write one fact about your drawing.

_____

Math Time

Work in your math curriculum for 30 to 40 min.

Check when done. ___

Relax for a while and watch a tutorial or documentary for 30 min.

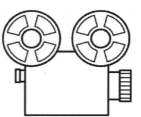 Movie Review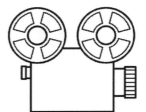

Write one thing you learned.

_____

Rate this movie. Color the stars.
5 stars mean it was Awesome!

Draw a scene from the movie.

Bible Time

Read for 15 min. in your bible.

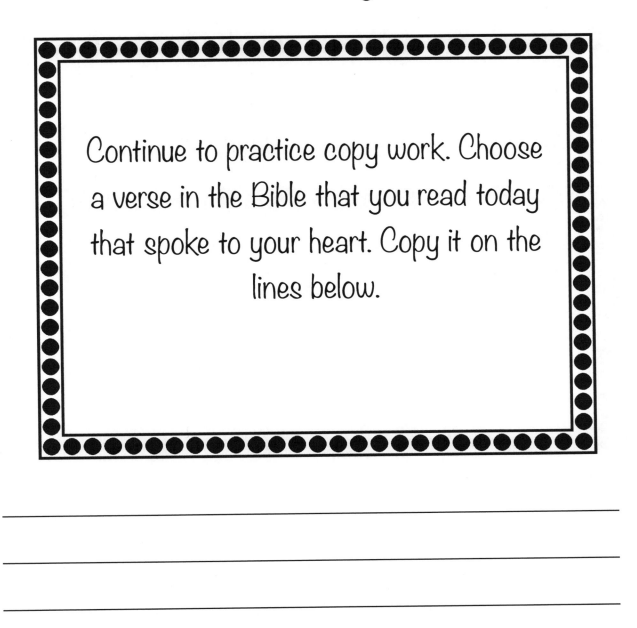

Continue to practice copy work. Choose a verse in the Bible that you read today that spoke to your heart. Copy it on the lines below.

_____

_____

_____

_____

_____

Reading and Language

Choose one of your classic novels to read.
(Read 5 pages)
Copy a paragraph from your book and circle all the nouns.

Remember a noun is a......person,place,thing, or idea !

_____

_____

_____

_____

_____

Did you put a capital letter at the beginning of your
sentences and punctuation at the end?

Historical Figure Book

(Read 5 to 10 pages)

Title:_____Author:_____

Draw a portrait of your historical figure.

A Time In History

After looking at pictures and learning about different people , places and things in history lets learn about dates in history.

Write Todays Date

_____

Look up what important thing happened in history on this day?

_____

_____

_____

Draw a picture of what happened.

Nature Study

Draw something in nature. Write one fact about your drawing.

_____

Math Time

Work in your math curriculum for 30 to 40 min.

Check when done. ___

Relax for a while and watch a tutorial or documentary for 30 min.

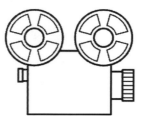 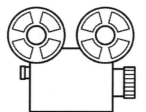

Movie Review

Write one thing you learned.

_____

Rate this movie. Color the stars.
5 stars mean it was Awesome!

Draw a scene from the movie.

Date : _____   Day 64

Bible Time

Read for 15 min. in your bible.

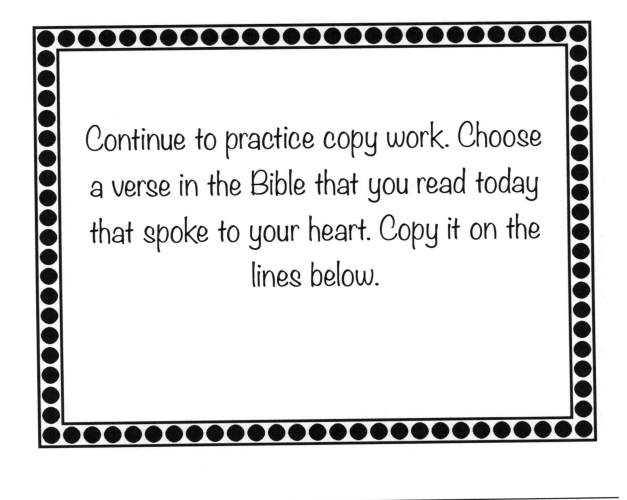

Continue to practice copy work. Choose a verse in the Bible that you read today that spoke to your heart. Copy it on the lines below.

_____

_____

_____

_____

Reading and Language

Choose one of your classic novels to read.

(Read 5 pages)

Copy a paragraph from your book and circle all the verbs.

Remember a verb is an......action word !

_____

_____

_____

_____

_____

Did you put a capital letter at the beginning of your
sentences and punctuation at the end?

Historical Figure Book

(Read 5 to 10 pages)

Title:_____Author:_____

Where does your story take place? Describe what the place looks like then draw a picture.

_____

_____

_____

_____

A Time In History

After looking at pictures and learning about different people , places and things in history lets learn about dates in history.

Write Todays Date

_____

Look up what important thing happened in history on this day?

_____

_____

_____

Draw a picture of what happened.

Nature Study

Draw something in nature. Write one fact about your drawing.

_____

Math Time

Work in your math curriculum for 30 to 40 min.

Check when done. ___

Relax for a while and watch a tutorial or documentary for 30 min.

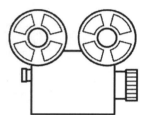 Movie Review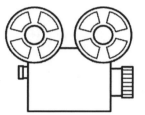

Write one thing you learned.

_____

Rate this movie. Color the stars.
5 stars mean it was Awesome!

Draw a scene from the movie.

Date :_____   Day 65

Bible Time

Read for 15 min. in your bible.

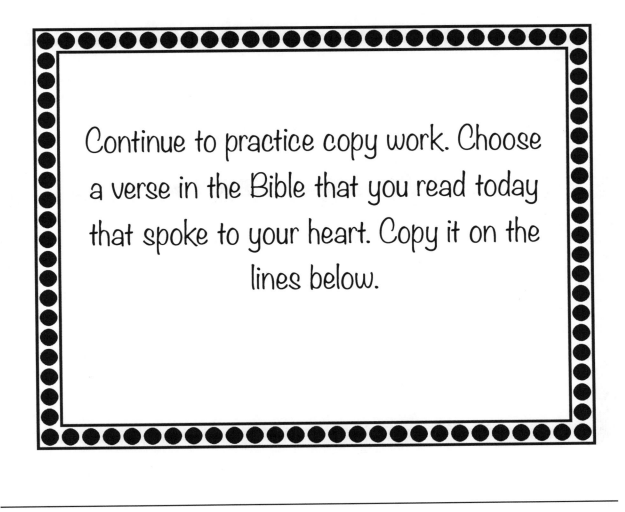

Continue to practice copy work. Choose a verse in the Bible that you read today that spoke to your heart. Copy it on the lines below.

_____

_____

_____

_____

Reading and Language

Choose one of your classic novels to read.
(Read 5 pages)
Copy a paragraph from your book and circle all the adjectives.

Remember an adjective is a......describing word !

_____

_____

_____

_____

_____

Did you put a capital letter at the beginning of your
sentences and punctuation at the end?

Historical Figure Book

(Read 5 to 10 pages)

Title:_____ Author:_____

What is this person famous for? Draw a picture of what they are famous for.

_____

_____

A Time In History

After looking at pictures and learning about different people , places and things in history lets learn about dates in history.

Write Todays Date

_____

Look up what important thing happened in history on this day?

_____

_____

_____

Draw a picture of what happened.

Nature Study

Draw something in nature. Write one fact about your drawing.

_____

Math Time

Work in your math curriculum for 30 to 40 min.

Check when done. ___

Relax for a while and watch a tutorial or documentary for 30 min.

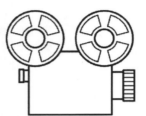 Movie Review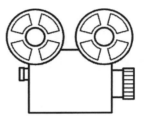

Write one thing you learned.

_____

Rate this movie. Color the stars.
5 stars mean it was Awesome!

Draw a scene from the movie.

Date : _____

Bible Time

Read for 15 min. in your bible.

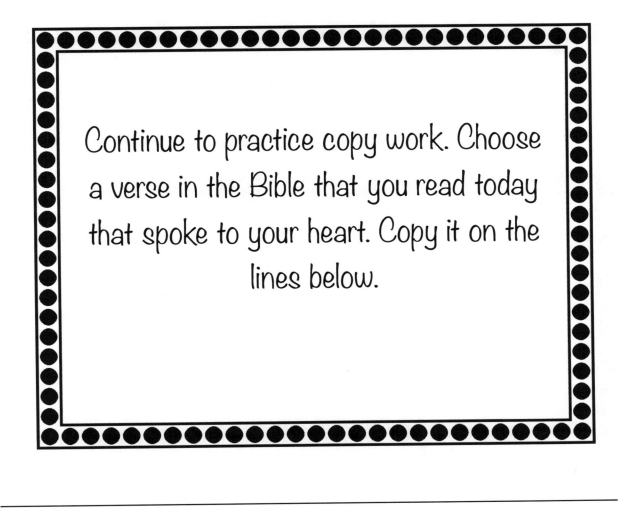

Continue to practice copy work. Choose a verse in the Bible that you read today that spoke to your heart. Copy it on the lines below.

_____

_____

_____

_____

Reading and Language

Choose one of your classic novels to read.

(Read 5 pages)

Copy a paragraph from your book and circle all the nouns.

Remember a noun is a......person,place,thing, or idea !

_____

_____

_____

_____

_____

Did you put a capital letter at the beginning of your
sentences and punctuation at the end?

Historical Figure Book

(Read 5 to 10 pages)

Title:_____Author:_____

What is the most interesting thing you learned?

_____

_____

_____

List four words to describe this person.

_____

_____

_____

_____

A Time In History

After looking at pictures and learning about different people , places and things in history lets learn about dates in history.

Write Todays Date

_____

Look up what important thing happened in history on this day?

_____

_____

_____

Draw a picture of what happened.

Nature Study

Draw something in nature. Write one fact about your drawing.

_____

Math Time

Work in your math curriculum for 30 to 40 min.

Check when done. ___

Relax for a while and watch a tutorial or documentary for 30 min.

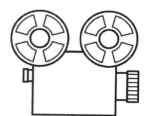 Movie Review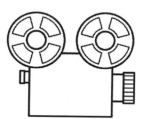

Write one thing you learned.

_____

Rate this movie. Color the stars.
5 stars mean it was Awesome!

Draw a scene from the movie.

Bible Time

Read for 15 min. in your bible.

Continue to practice copy work. Choose a verse in the Bible that you read today that spoke to your heart. Copy it on the lines below.

_____

_____

_____

_____

Reading and Language

Choose one of your classic novels to read.
(Read 5 pages)
Copy a paragraph from your book and circle all
the verbs.

Remember a verb is an......action word !

_____

_____

_____

_____

_____

_____

Did you put a capital letter at the beginning of your
sentences and punctuation at the end?

Historical Figure Book

(Read 5 to 10 pages)

Title:_____Author:_____

Tell in your own words what you read.

_____

_____

_____

_____

_____

_____

_____

_____

_____

A Time In History

After looking at pictures and learning about different people , places and things in history lets learn about dates in history.

Write Todays Date

_____

Look up what important thing happened in history on this day?

_____

_____

_____

Draw a picture of what happened.

Nature Study

Draw something in nature. Write one fact about your drawing.

_____

Math Time

Work in your math curriculum for 30 to 40 min.

Check when done. ___

Relax for a while and watch a tutorial or documentary for 30 min.

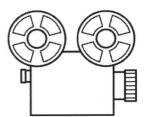
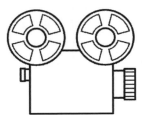

Movie Review

Write one thing you learned.

_____

Rate this movie. Color the stars.
5 stars mean it was Awesome!

Draw a scene from the movie.

Date : _____

Bible Time

Read for 15 min. in your bible.

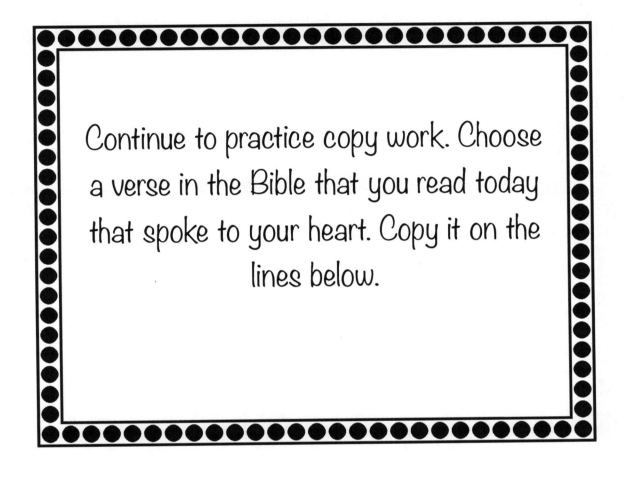

Continue to practice copy work. Choose a verse in the Bible that you read today that spoke to your heart. Copy it on the lines below.

_____

_____

_____

_____

Reading and Language

Choose one of your classic novels to read.

(Read 5 pages)

Copy a paragraph from your book and circle all the adjectives.

Remember an adjective is a......describing word !

_____

_____

_____

_____

_____

Did you put a capital letter at the beginning of your sentences and punctuation at the end?

Historical Figure Book

(Read 5 to 10 pages)

Title:_____Author:_____

Tell in your own words what you read.

_____

_____

_____

_____

_____

_____

_____

_____

_____

_____

A Time In History

After looking at pictures and learning about different people , places and things in history lets learn about dates in history.

Write Todays Date

_____

Look up what important thing happened in history on this day?

_____

_____

_____

Draw a picture of what happened.

Nature Study

Draw something in nature. Write one fact about your drawing.

_____

Math Time

Work in your math curriculum for 30 to 40 min.

Check when done. ___

Relax for a while and watch a tutorial or documentary for 30 min.

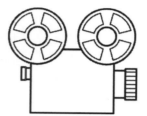
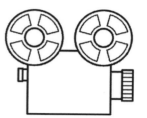

Movie Review

Write one thing you learned.

_____

Rate this movie. Color the stars.
5 stars mean it was Awesome!

Draw a scene from the movie.

Bible Time

Read for 15 min. in your bible.

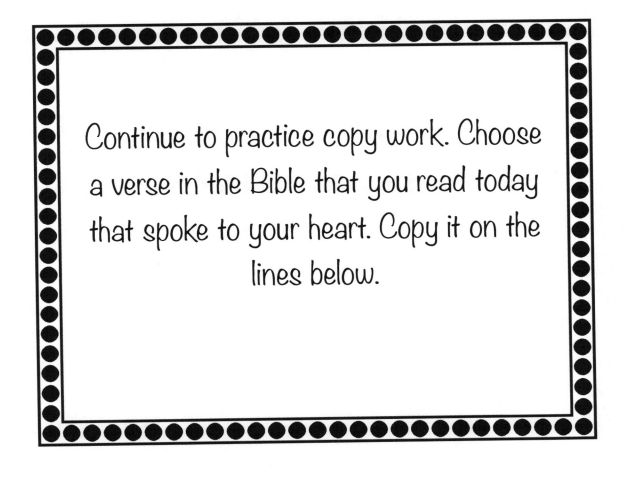

Continue to practice copy work. Choose a verse in the Bible that you read today that spoke to your heart. Copy it on the lines below.

_____

_____

_____

_____

_____

Reading and Language

Choose one of your classic novels to read.
(Read 5 pages)

Copy a paragraph from your book and circle all the nouns.

Remember a noun is a......person,place,thing, or idea !

Did you put a capital letter at the beginning of your sentences and punctuation at the end?

Historical Figure Book

(Read 5 to 10 pages)

Title:_____ Author:_____

Tell me about this persons character.

_____

_____

_____

Do you think this is a person you would like to be
friends with?

_____

_____

_____

_____

_____

A Time In History

After looking at pictures and learning about different people , places and things in history lets learn about dates in history.

Write Todays Date

_____

Look up what important thing happened in history on this day?

_____

_____

_____

Draw a picture of what happened.

Nature Study

Draw something in nature. Write one fact about your drawing.

_____

Math Time

Work in your math curriculum for 30 to 40 min.

Check when done. ___

Relax for a while and watch a tutorial or documentary for 30 min.

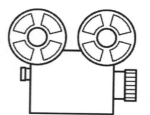 Movie Review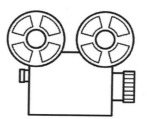

Write one thing you learned.

_____

Rate this movie. Color the stars.
5 stars mean it was Awesome!

Draw a scene from the movie.

Bible Time

Read for 15 min. in your bible.

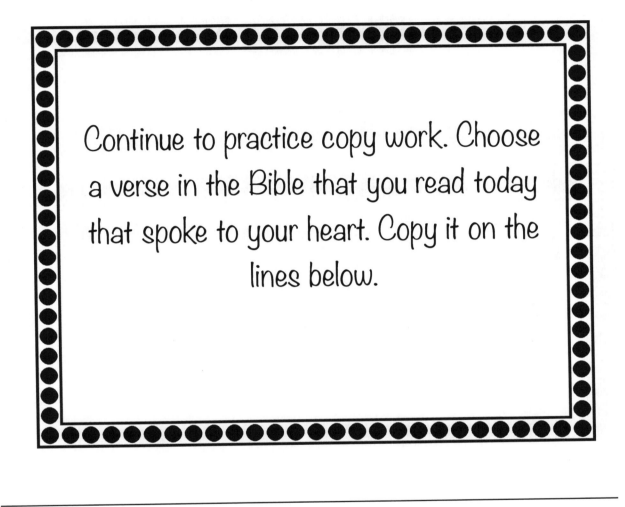

Continue to practice copy work. Choose a verse in the Bible that you read today that spoke to your heart. Copy it on the lines below.

_____

_____

_____

_____

_____

Reading and Language

Choose one of your classic novels to read.

(Read 5 pages)

Copy a paragraph from your book and circle all the verbs.

Remember a verb is an......action word !

_____

_____

_____

_____

_____

Did you put a capital letter at the beginning of your
sentences and punctuation at the end?

Historical Figure Book

(Read 5 to 10 pages)

Title:_____Author:_____

Do you think you could live during the time of your historical figure? Tell why or why not.

_____

_____

_____

_____

_____

_____

_____

_____

_____

A Time In History

After looking at pictures and learning about different people , places and things in history lets learn about dates in history.

Write Todays Date

_____

Look up what important thing happened in history on this day?

_____

_____

_____

Draw a picture of what happened.

Nature Study

Draw something in nature. Write one fact about your drawing.

_____

Math Time

Work in your math curriculum for 30 to 40 min.

Check when done. ___

Relax for a while and watch a tutorial or documentary for 30 min.

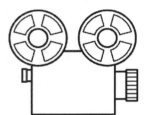 Movie Review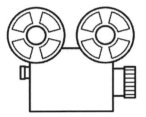

Write one thing you learned.

_____

Rate this movie. Color the stars.
5 stars mean it was Awesome!

Draw a scene from the movie.

Date : _____   Day 71

Bible Time

Read for 15 min. in your bible.

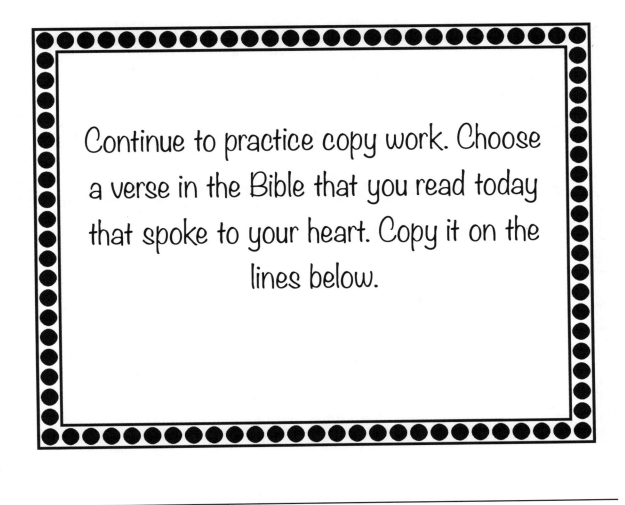

Continue to practice copy work. Choose a verse in the Bible that you read today that spoke to your heart. Copy it on the lines below.

_____

_____

_____

_____

_____

Reading and Language

Choose one of your classic novels to read.
(Read 5 pages)

Copy a paragraph from your book and circle all the adjectives.

Remember an adjective is a.....describing word !

Did you put a capital letter at the beginning of your sentences and punctuation at the end?

Historical Figure Book

(Read 5 to 10 pages)

Title:_____Author:_____

What era is this person from?

Draw the type of clothing they wore or wear.

_____

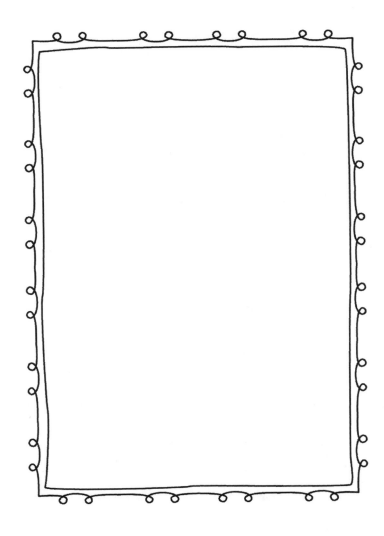

A Time In History

After looking at pictures and learning about different people , places and things in history lets learn about dates in history.

Write Todays Date

_____

Look up what important thing happened in history on this day?

_____

_____

_____

Draw a picture of what happened.

Nature Study

Draw something in nature. Write one fact about your drawing.

_____

Math Time

Work in your math curriculum for 30 to 40 min.

Check when done. ___

Relax for a while and watch a tutorial or documentary for 30 min.

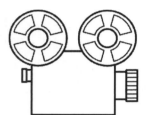 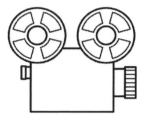

<u>Movie Review</u>

Write one thing you learned.

_____

Rate this movie. Color the stars.
5 stars mean it was Awesome!

Draw a scene from the movie.

Date :_____

Bible Time

Read for 15 min. in your bible.

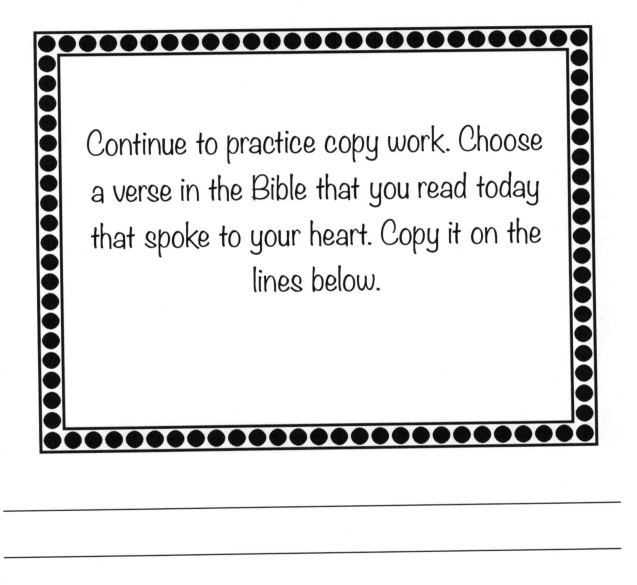

Continue to practice copy work. Choose a verse in the Bible that you read today that spoke to your heart. Copy it on the lines below.

_____

_____

_____

_____

Reading and Language

Choose one of your classic novels to read.

(Read 5 pages)

Copy a paragraph from your book and circle all the nouns.

Remember a noun is a......person,place,thing, or idea !

_____

_____

_____

_____

_____

_____

Did you put a capital letter at the beginning of your sentences and punctuation at the end?

Historical Figure Book

(Read 5 to 10 pages)

Title:_____Author:_____

Tell in your own words what you read today.

_____

_____

_____

_____

_____

_____

_____

_____

A Time In History

After looking at pictures and learning about different people , places and things in history lets learn about dates in history.

Write Todays Date

_____

Look up what important thing happened in history on this day?

_____

_____

_____

Draw a picture of what happened.

Nature Study

Draw something in nature. Write one fact about your drawing.

_____

Math Time

Work in your math curriculum for 30 to 40 min.

Check when done. ___

Relax for a while and watch a tutorial or documentary for 30 min.

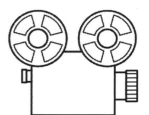

Movie Review

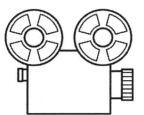

Write one thing you learned.

_____

Rate this movie. Color the stars.
5 stars mean it was Awesome!

Draw a scene from the movie.

Date : _____   Day 73

Bible Time

Read for 15 min. in your bible.

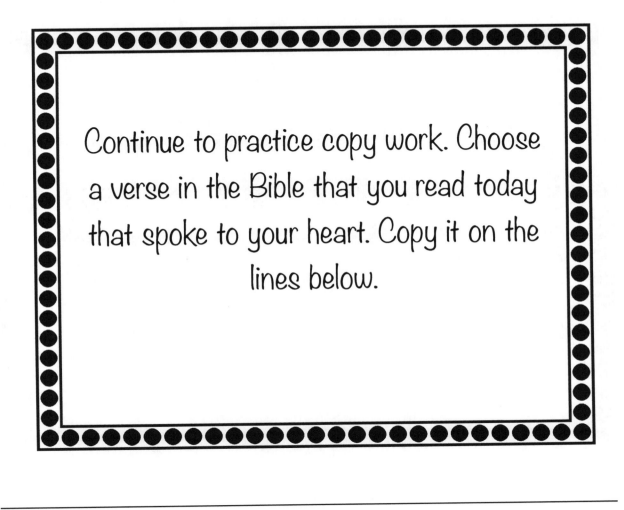

Continue to practice copy work. Choose a verse in the Bible that you read today that spoke to your heart. Copy it on the lines below.

_____

_____

_____

_____

_____

Reading and Language

Choose one of your classic novels to read.

(Read 5 pages)

Copy a paragraph from your book and circle all the verbs.

Remember a verb is an......action word !

_____

_____

_____

_____

_____

Did you put a capital letter at the beginning of your sentences and punctuation at the end?

Historical Figure Book

(Read 5 to 10 pages)

Title:_____Author:_____

Did this person face any struggles during their life if
so what were the struggles?

_____

_____

_____

_____

_____

How did they over come their struggles?

_____

_____

_____

_____

A Time In History

After looking at pictures and learning about different people , places and things in history lets learn about dates in history.

Write Todays Date

_____

Look up what important thing happened in history on this day?

_____

_____

_____

Draw a picture of what happened.

Nature Study

Draw something in nature. Write one fact about your drawing.

_____

Math Time

Work in your math curriculum for 30 to 40 min.

Check when done. ___

Relax for a while and watch a tutorial or documentary for 30 min.

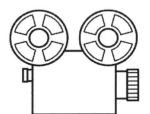

<u>Movie Review</u>

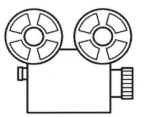

Write one thing you learned.

Rate this movie. Color the stars.
5 stars mean it was Awesome!

Draw a scene from the movie.

Date :_____   Day 74

Bible Time

Read for 15 min. in your bible.

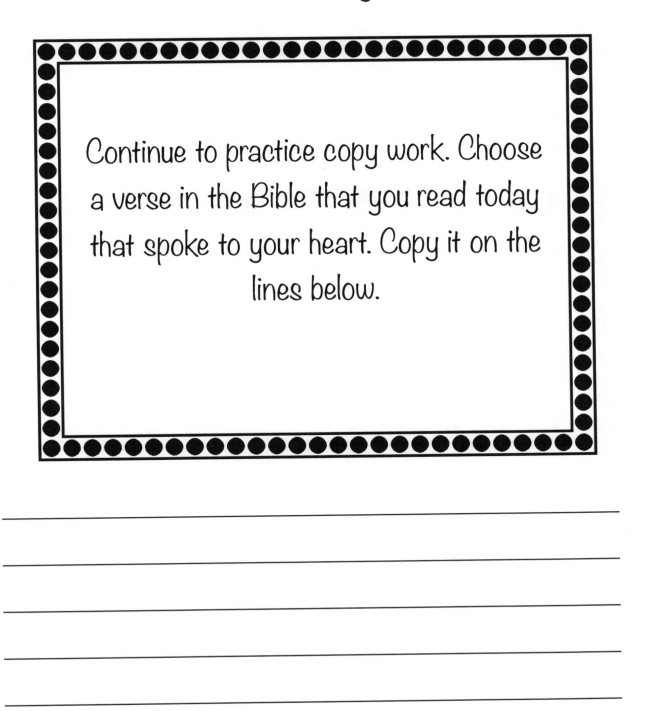

Continue to practice copy work. Choose a verse in the Bible that you read today that spoke to your heart. Copy it on the lines below.

_____

_____

_____

_____

Reading and Language

Choose one of your classic novels to read.

(Read 5 pages)

Copy a paragraph from your book and circle all the adjectives.

Remember an adjective is a......describing word !

Did you put a capital letter at the beginning of your sentences and punctuation at the end?

Historical Figure Book

(Read 5 to 10 pages)

Title:_____Author:_____

Tell about this persons education. Did they go to school? Draw a picture of what school might have looked like for them.

_____

_____

_____

_____

A Time In History

After looking at pictures and learning about different people , places and things in history lets learn about dates in history.

Write Todays Date

_____

Look up what important thing happened in history on this day?

_____

_____

_____

Draw a picture of what happened.

Nature Study

Draw something in nature. Write one fact about your drawing.

_____

Math Time

Work in your math curriculum for 30 to 40 min.

Check when done. ___

Relax for a while and watch a tutorial or documentary for 30 min.

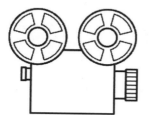 Movie Review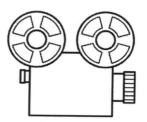

Write one thing you learned.

_____

Rate this movie. Color the stars.
5 stars mean it was Awesome!

Draw a scene from the movie.

Date : _____

Bible Time

Read for 15 min. in your bible.

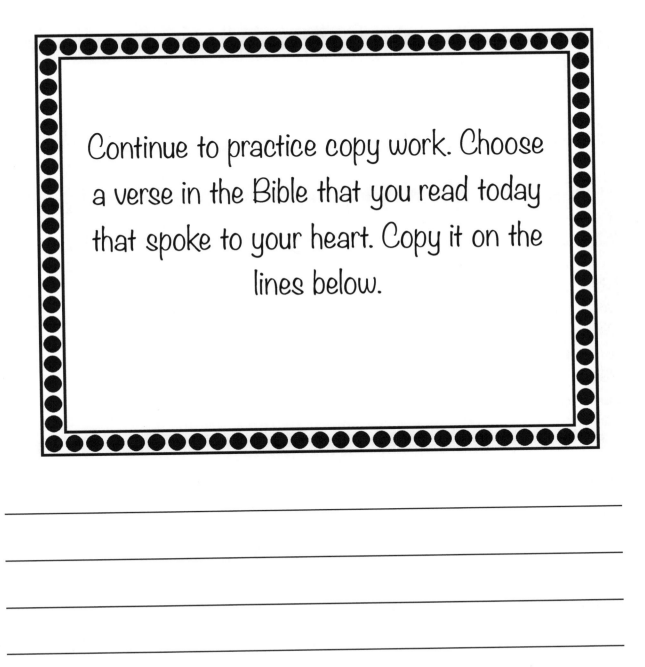

Continue to practice copy work. Choose a verse in the Bible that you read today that spoke to your heart. Copy it on the lines below.

_____

_____

_____

_____

_____

Reading and Language

Choose one of your classic novels to read.

(Read 5 pages)

Copy a paragraph from your book and circle all the nouns.

Remember a noun is a......person, place, thing, or idea !

_____

_____

_____

_____

_____

Did you put a capital letter at the beginning of your
sentences and punctuation at the end?

Historical Figure Book

(Read 5 to 10 pages)

Title:_____Author:_____

Draw a picture of a scene from your book.

A Time In History

After looking at pictures and learning about different people , places and things in history lets learn about dates in history.

Write Todays Date

_____

Look up what important thing happened in history on this day?

_____

_____

_____

Draw a picture of what happened.

Nature Study

Draw something in nature. Write one fact about your drawing.

_____

Math Time

Work in your math curriculum for 30 to 40 min.

Check when done. ___

Relax for a while and watch a tutorial or documentary for 30 min.

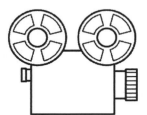

Movie Review

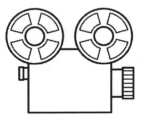

Write one thing you learned.

_____

Rate this movie. Color the stars.
5 stars mean it was Awesome!

Draw a scene from the movie.

Bible Time

Read for 15 min. in your bible.

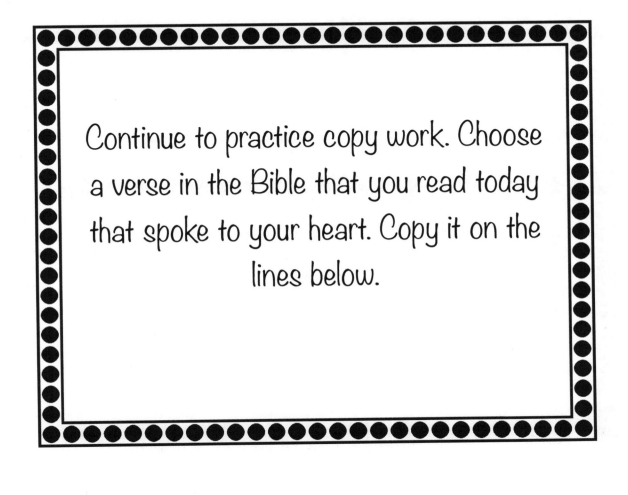

Continue to practice copy work. Choose a verse in the Bible that you read today that spoke to your heart. Copy it on the lines below.

_____

_____

_____

_____

_____

Reading and Language

Choose one of your classic novels to read.
(Read 5 pages)
Copy a paragraph from your book and circle all the verbs.

Remember a verb is an......action word !

_____

_____

_____

_____

_____

Did you put a capital letter at the beginning of your sentences and punctuation at the end?

Historical Figure Book

(Read 5 to 10 pages)

Title:_____Author:_____

If you could ask this person anything what would you ask?

_____

_____

Design a postage stamp in honor of this person.

A Time In History

After looking at pictures and learning about different people , places and things in history lets learn about dates in history.

Write Todays Date

_____

Look up what important thing happened in history on this day?

_____

_____

_____

Draw a picture of what happened.

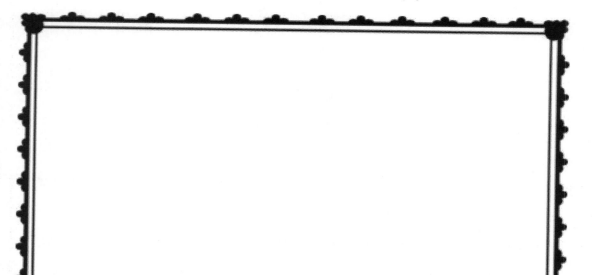

Nature Study

Draw something in nature. Write one fact about your drawing.

_____

Math Time

Work in your math curriculum for 30 to 40 min.

Check when done. ___

Relax for a while and watch a tutorial or documentary for 30 min.

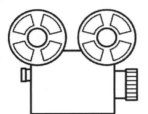 Movie Review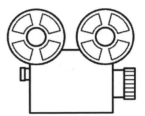

Write one thing you learned.

_____

Rate this movie. Color the stars.
5 stars mean it was Awesome!

Draw a scene from the movie.

Date :＿＿＿＿＿＿＿＿＿

Bible Time

Read for 15 min. in your bible.

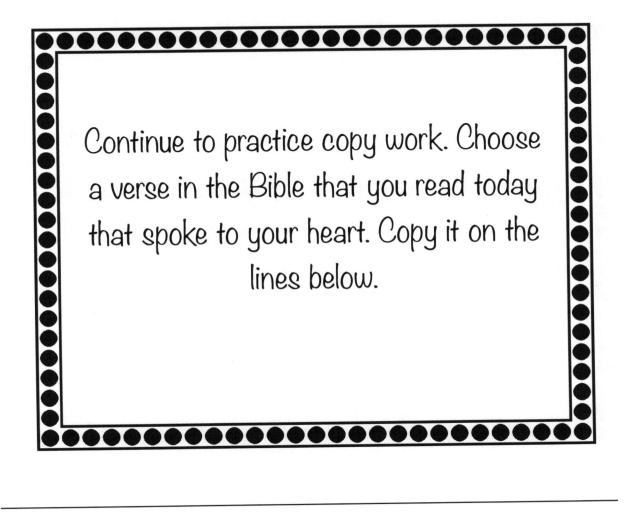

Continue to practice copy work. Choose a verse in the Bible that you read today that spoke to your heart. Copy it on the lines below.

＿＿＿＿＿＿＿＿＿＿＿＿＿＿＿＿＿＿＿＿＿

＿＿＿＿＿＿＿＿＿＿＿＿＿＿＿＿＿＿＿＿＿

＿＿＿＿＿＿＿＿＿＿＿＿＿＿＿＿＿＿＿＿＿

＿＿＿＿＿＿＿＿＿＿＿＿＿＿＿＿＿＿＿＿＿

Reading and Language

Choose one of your classic novels to read.

(Read 5 pages)

Copy a paragraph from your book and circle all the adjectives.

Remember an adjective is a......describing word !

_____

_____

_____

_____

_____

Did you put a capital letter at the beginning of your
sentences and punctuation at the end?

Historical Figure Book

(Read 5 to 10 pages)

Title:_____Author:_____

Tell in your own words what you read today.

_____

_____

_____

_____

_____

_____

_____

_____

A Time In History

After looking at pictures and learning about different people , places and things in history lets learn about dates in history.

Write Todays Date

_____

Look up what important thing happened in history on this day?

_____

_____

_____

Draw a picture of what happened.

Nature Study

Draw something in nature. Write one fact about your drawing.

_____

Math Time

Work in your math curriculum for 30 to 40 min.

Check when done. ___

Relax for a while and watch a tutorial or documentary for 30 min.

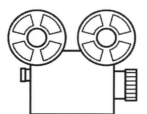 **Movie Review**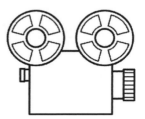

Write one thing you learned.

_____

Rate this movie. Color the stars.
5 stars mean it was Awesome!

Draw a scene from the movie.

Date :_____

Bible Time

Read for 15 min. in your bible.

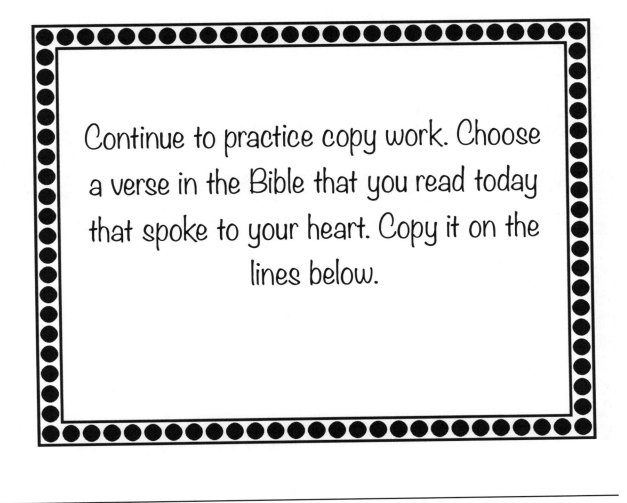

Continue to practice copy work. Choose a verse in the Bible that you read today that spoke to your heart. Copy it on the lines below.

_____

_____

_____

_____

Reading and Language

Choose one of your classic novels to read.

(Read 5 pages)

Copy a paragraph from your book and circle all the nouns.

Remember a noun is a......person, place, thing, or idea !

_____

_____

_____

_____

_____

Did you put a capital letter at the beginning of your
sentences and punctuation at the end?

Historical Figure Book

(Read 5 to 10 pages)

Title:_____Author:_____

How did this person die? Or if still alive what are they doing now?

_____

_____

_____

_____

_____

_____

_____

Draw a picture.

A Time In History

After looking at pictures and learning about different people , places and things in history lets learn about dates in history.

Write Todays Date

_____

Look up what important thing happened in history on this day?

_____

_____

_____

Draw a picture of what happened.

Nature Study

Draw something in nature. Write one fact about your drawing.

_____

Math Time

Work in your math curriculum for 30 to 40 min.

Check when done. ___

Relax for a while and watch a tutorial or documentary for 30 min.

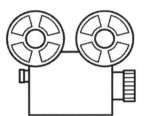 Movie Review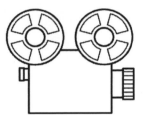

Write one thing you learned.

_____

Rate this movie. Color the stars.
5 stars mean it was Awesome!

Draw a scene from the movie.

Bible Time

Read for 15 min. in your bible.

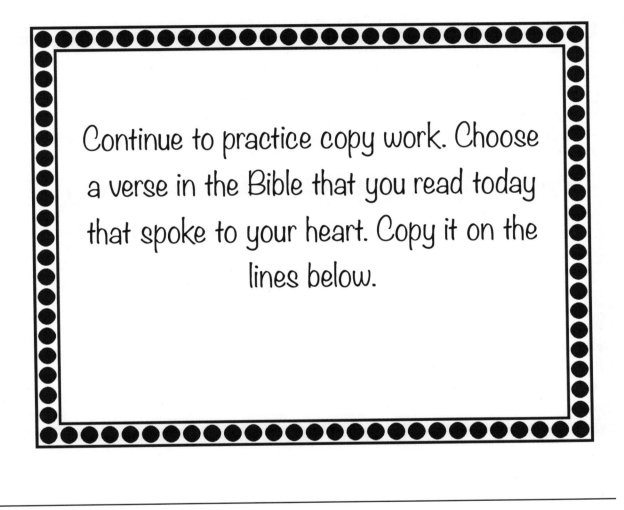

Continue to practice copy work. Choose a verse in the Bible that you read today that spoke to your heart. Copy it on the lines below.

_____

_____

_____

_____

Reading and Language

Choose one of your classic novels to read.

(Read 5 pages)

Copy a paragraph from your book and circle all the verbs.

Remember a verb is an......action word !

_____

_____

_____

_____

_____

Did you put a capital letter at the beginning of your sentences and punctuation at the end?

Historical Figure Book

(Read 5 to 10 pages)

Title:_____Author:_____

Did you like learning about this person?
Tell why or why not.

_____

_____

_____

_____

_____

_____

_____

_____

_____

_____

A Time In History

After looking at pictures and learning about different people , places and things in history lets learn about dates in history.

Write Todays Date

_____

Look up what important thing happened in history on this day?

_____

_____

_____

Draw a picture of what happened.

Nature Study

Draw something in nature. Write one fact about your drawing.

_____

Math Time

Work in your math curriculum for 30 to 40 min.

Check when done. ___

Relax for a while and watch a tutorial or documentary for 30 min.

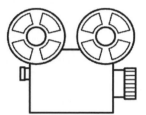 Movie Review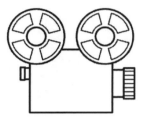

Write one thing you learned.

_____

Rate this movie. Color the stars.
5 stars mean it was Awesome!

Draw a scene from the movie.

Date : _____   Day 80

Bible Time

Read for 15 min. in your bible.

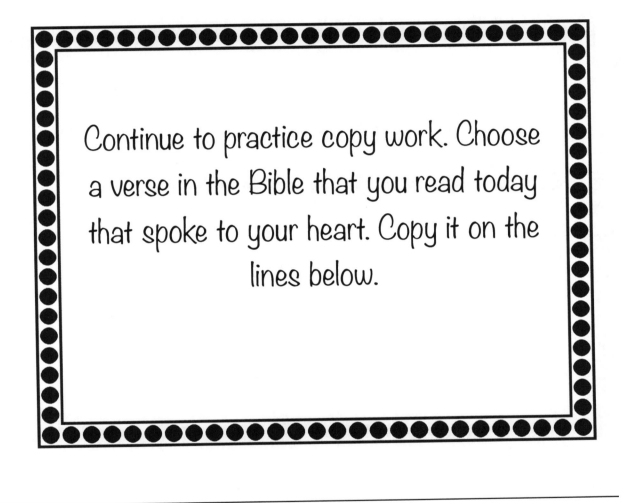

Continue to practice copy work. Choose
a verse in the Bible that you read today
that spoke to your heart. Copy it on the
lines below.

_____

_____

_____

_____

_____

Reading and Language

Choose one of your classic novels to read.

(Read 5 pages)

Copy a paragraph from your book and circle all the adjectives.

Remember an adjective is a......describing word !

_____

_____

_____

_____

_____

Did you put a capital letter at the beginning of your sentences and punctuation at the end?

Historical Figure Book

(Read 5 to 10 pages)

Title:_____Author:_____

Would you recommend this book to someone else?
Tell why you would recommend it.

_____

_____

_____

_____

_____

_____

_____

_____

_____

A Time In History

After looking at pictures and learning about different people , places and things in history lets learn about dates in history.

Write Todays Date

_____

Look up what important thing happened in history on this day?

_____

_____

_____

Draw a picture of what happened.

Nature Study

Draw something in nature. Write one fact about your drawing.

_____

Math Time

Work in your math curriculum for 30 to 40 min.

Check when done. ___

Relax for a while and watch a tutorial or documentary for 30 min.

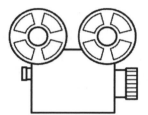

Movie Review

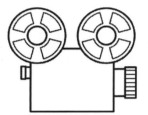

Write one thing you learned.

_____

Rate this movie. Color the stars.
5 stars mean it was Awesome!

Draw a scene from the movie.

Bible Time

Read for 15 min. in your bible.

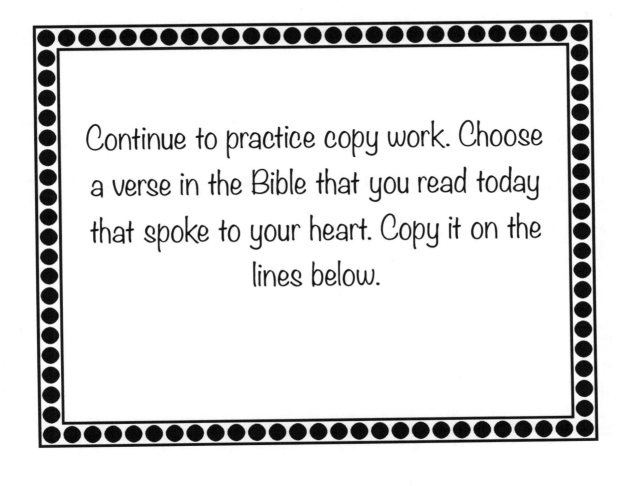

Continue to practice copy work. Choose a verse in the Bible that you read today that spoke to your heart. Copy it on the lines below.

_____

_____

_____

_____

_____

Reading and Language

Choose one of your classic novels to read.

(Read 5 pages)

Copy a paragraph from your book and circle all the nouns.

Remember a noun is a......person,place,thing, or idea !

_____

_____

_____

_____

_____

Did you put a capital letter at the beginning of your
sentences and punctuation at the end?

Historical Figure Book

(Read 5 to 10 pages)

Title:_____Author:_____

Who are you reading about?

_____

Where are they from?

_____

Color the map where this person lived or lives. A Time In History

A Time In History

After looking at pictures and learning about different people , places and things in history lets learn about dates in history.

Write Todays Date

_____

Look up what important thing happened in history on this day?

_____

_____

_____

Draw a picture of what happened.

Nature Study

Draw something in nature. Write one fact about your drawing.

_____

Math Time

Work in your math curriculum for 30 to 40 min.

Check when done. ___

Relax for a while and watch a tutorial or documentary for 30 min.

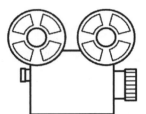

Movie Review

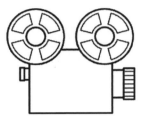

Write one thing you learned.

_____

Rate this movie. Color the stars.
5 stars mean it was Awesome!

Draw a scene from the movie.

Bible Time

Read for 15 min. in your bible.

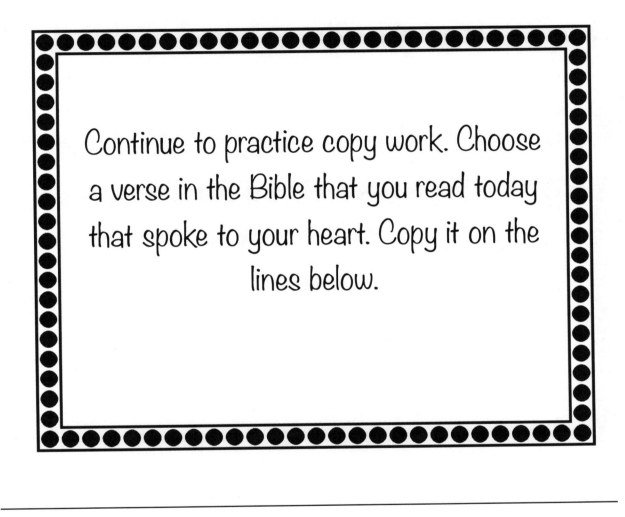

Continue to practice copy work. Choose a verse in the Bible that you read today that spoke to your heart. Copy it on the lines below.

_____

_____

_____

_____

Reading and Language

Choose one of your classic novels to read.

(Read 5 pages)

Copy a paragraph from your book and circle all the verbs.

Remember a verb is an......action word !

_____

_____

_____

_____

_____

Did you put a capital letter at the beginning of your sentences and punctuation at the end?

Historical Figure Book

(Read 5 to 10 pages)

Title:_____Author:_____

Tell in your own words what you read today.

_____

_____

_____

_____

_____

_____

_____

When did this person live or if still alive, when was this person born?

_____

A Time In History

After looking at pictures and learning about different people , places and things in history lets learn about dates in history.

Write Todays Date

_____

Look up what important thing happened in history on this day?

_____

_____

_____

Draw a picture of what happened.

Nature Study

Draw something in nature. Write one fact about your drawing.

_____

Math Time

Work in your math curriculum for 30 to 40 min.

Check when done. ___

Relax for a while and watch a tutorial or documentary for 30 min.

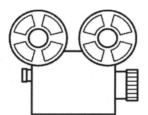 <u>Movie Review</u>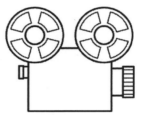

Write one thing you learned.

_____

Rate this movie. Color the stars.
5 stars mean it was Awesome!

Draw a scene from the movie.

Date :_____   Day 83

Bible Time

Read for 15 min. in your bible.

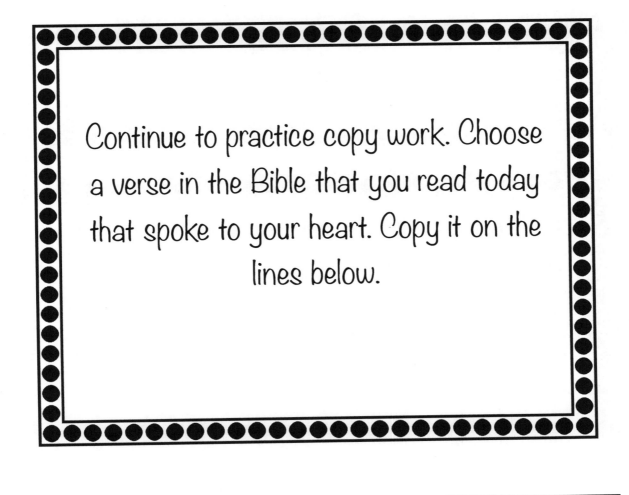

Continue to practice copy work. Choose a verse in the Bible that you read today that spoke to your heart. Copy it on the lines below.

_____

_____

_____

_____

_____

Reading and Language

Choose one of your classic novels to read.

(Read 5 pages)

Copy a paragraph from your book and circle all the adjectives.

Remember an adjective is a......describing word !

_____

_____

_____

_____

_____

Did you put a capital letter at the beginning of your sentences and punctuation at the end?

Historical Figure Book

(Read 5 to 10 pages)

Title:_____Author:_____

Draw a portrait of your historical figure.

A Time In History

After looking at pictures and learning about different people , places and things in history lets learn about dates in history.

Write Todays Date

_____

Look up what important thing happened in history on this day?

_____

_____

_____

Draw a picture of what happened.

Nature Study

Draw something in nature. Write one fact about your drawing.

_____

Math Time

Work in your math curriculum for 30 to 40 min.

Check when done. ___

Relax for a while and watch a tutorial or documentary for 30 min.

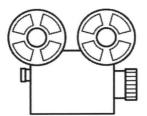 Movie Review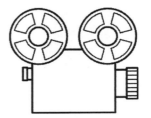

Write one thing you learned.

Rate this movie. Color the stars.
5 stars mean it was Awesome!

Draw a scene from the movie.

Date :_____   Day 84

Bible Time

Read for 15 min. in your bible.

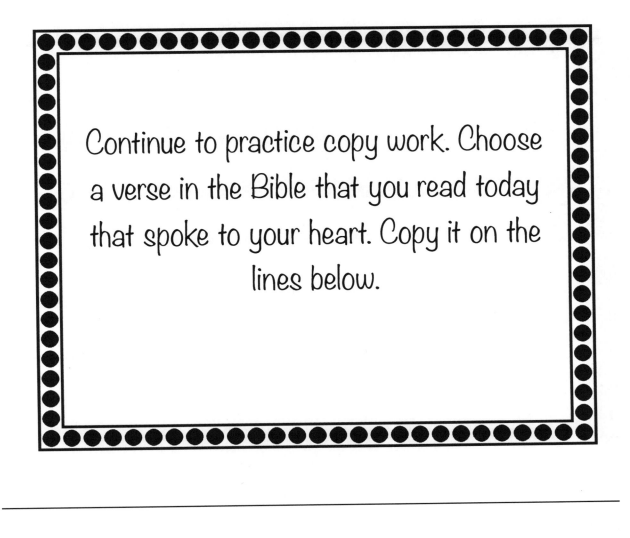

Continue to practice copy work. Choose a verse in the Bible that you read today that spoke to your heart. Copy it on the lines below.

_____

_____

_____

_____

_____

Reading and Language

Choose one of your classic novels to read.

(Read 5 pages)

Copy a paragraph from your book and circle all the nouns.

Remember a noun is a......person,place,thing, or idea !

_____

_____

_____

_____

_____

Did you put a capital letter at the beginning of your
sentences and punctuation at the end?

Historical Figure Book

(Read 5 to 10 pages)

Title:_____Author:_____

Where does your story take place? Describe what the
place looks like then draw a picture.

_____

_____

_____

_____

_____

A Time In History

After looking at pictures and learning about different people , places and things in history lets learn about dates in history.

Write Todays Date

_____

Look up what important thing happened in history on this day?

_____

_____

_____

Draw a picture of what happened.

Nature Study

Draw something in nature. Write one fact about your drawing.

_____

Math Time

Work in your math curriculum for 30 to 40 min.

Check when done. ___

Relax for a while and watch a tutorial or documentary for 30 min.

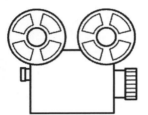 Movie Review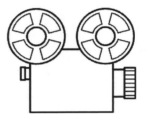

Write one thing you learned.

Rate this movie. Color the stars.
5 stars mean it was Awesome!

Draw a scene from the movie.

Date :_____

Bible Time

Read for 15 min. in your bible.

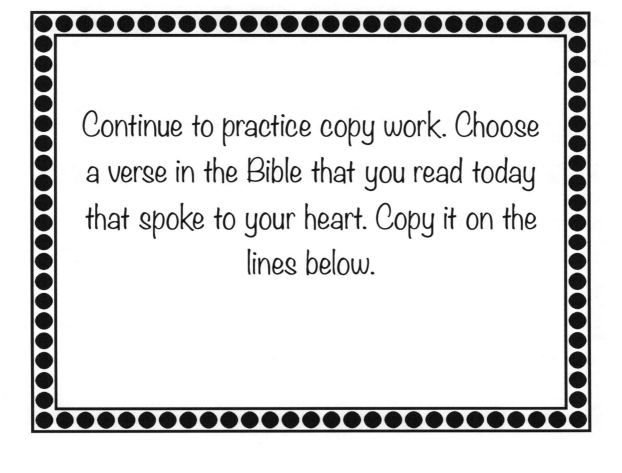

Continue to practice copy work. Choose
a verse in the Bible that you read today
that spoke to your heart. Copy it on the
lines below.

_____

_____

_____

_____

_____

Reading and Language

Choose one of your classic novels to read.

(Read 5 pages)

Copy a paragraph from your book and circle all the verbs.

Remember a verb is an......action word !

_____

_____

_____

_____

_____

Did you put a capital letter at the beginning of your sentences and punctuation at the end?

Historical Figure Book

(Read 5 to 10 pages)

Title:_____Author:_____

What is this person famous for?Draw a picture of
what they are famous for.

_____

_____

A Time In History

After looking at pictures and learning about different people , places and things in history lets learn about dates in history.

Write Todays Date

_____

Look up what important thing happened in history on this day?

_____

_____

_____

Draw a picture of what happened.

Nature Study

Draw something in nature. Write one fact about your drawing.

_____

Math Time

Work in your math curriculum for 30 to 40 min.

Check when done. ___

Relax for a while and watch a tutorial or documentary for 30 min.

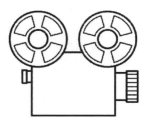 Movie Review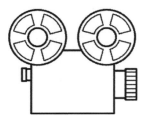

Write one thing you learned.

_____

Rate this movie. Color the stars.
5 stars mean it was Awesome!

Draw a scene from the movie.

Date :_____   Day 86

Bible Time

Read for 15 min. in your bible.

Continue to practice copy work. Choose a verse in the Bible that you read today that spoke to your heart. Copy it on the lines below.

_____

_____

_____

_____

_____

Reading and Language

Choose one of your classic novels to read.

(Read 5 pages)

Copy a paragraph from your book and circle all the adjectives.

Remember an adjective is a......describing word !

_____

_____

_____

_____

_____

Did you put a capital letter at the beginning of your
sentences and punctuation at the end?

Historical Figure Book

(Read 5 to 10 pages)

Title:_____Author:_____

What is the most interesting thing you learned?

_____

_____

_____

List four words to describe this person.

_____

_____

_____

_____

A Time In History

After looking at pictures and learning about different people , places and things in history lets learn about dates in history.

Write Todays Date

_____

Look up what important thing happened in history on this day?

_____

_____

_____

Draw a picture of what happened.

Nature Study

Draw something in nature. Write one fact about your drawing.

_____

Math Time

Work in your math curriculum for 30 to 40 min.

Check when done. ___

Relax for a while and watch a tutorial or documentary for 30 min.

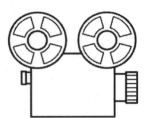 Movie Review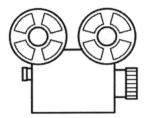

Write one thing you learned.

_____

Rate this movie. Color the stars.
5 stars mean it was Awesome!

Draw a scene from the movie.

Date :_____   Day 87

Bible Time

Read for 15 min. in your bible.

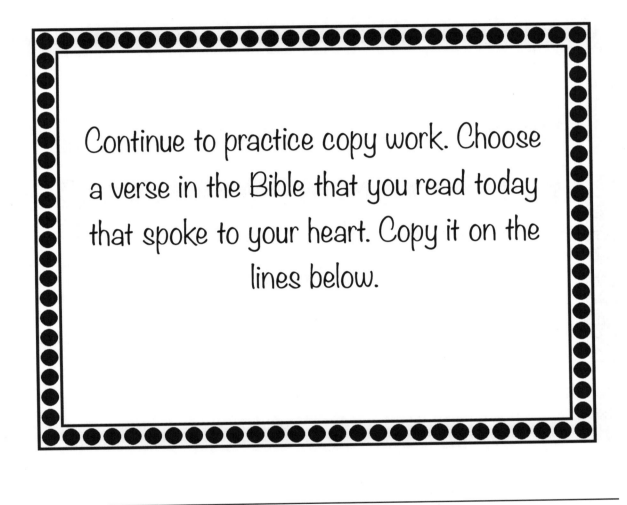

Continue to practice copy work. Choose a verse in the Bible that you read today that spoke to your heart. Copy it on the lines below.

_____

_____

_____

_____

Reading and Language

Choose one of your classic novels to read.
(Read 5 pages)
Copy a paragraph from your book and circle all the nouns.

Remember a noun is a......person,place,thing, or idea !

_____

_____

_____

_____

_____

Did you put a capital letter at the beginning of your
sentences and punctuation at the end?

Historical Figure Book
(Read 5 to 10 pages)

Title:_____Author:_____

Tell in your own words what you read.

_____

_____

_____

_____

_____

_____

_____

_____

_____

_____

A Time In History

After looking at pictures and learning about different people , places and things in history lets learn about dates in history.

Write Todays Date

_____

Look up what important thing happened in history on this day?

_____

_____

_____

Draw a picture of what happened.

Nature Study

Draw something in nature. Write one fact about your drawing.

_____

Math Time

Work in your math curriculum for 30 to 40 min.

Check when done. ___

Relax for a while and watch a tutorial or documentary for 30 min.

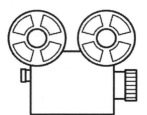 Movie Review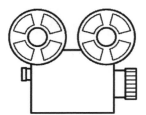

Write one thing you learned.

_____

Rate this movie. Color the stars.
5 stars mean it was Awesome!

Draw a scene from the movie.

Bible Time

Read for 15 min. in your bible.

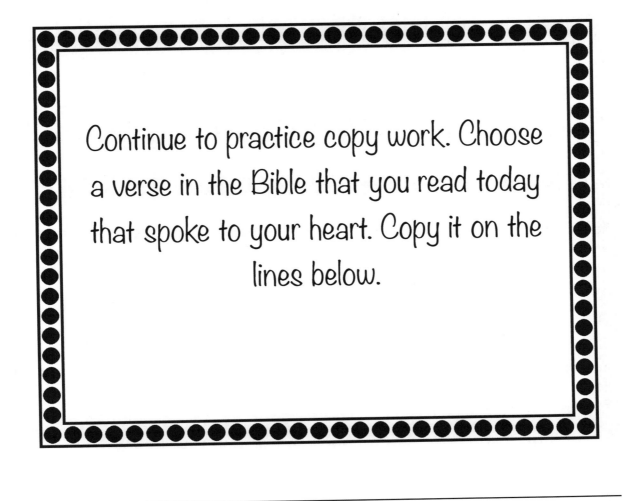

Continue to practice copy work. Choose
a verse in the Bible that you read today
that spoke to your heart. Copy it on the
lines below.

_____

_____

_____

_____

_____

Reading and Language

Choose one of your classic novels to read.
(Read 5 pages)
Copy a paragraph from your book and circle all the verbs.

Remember a verb is an......action word !

_____

_____

_____

_____

_____

Did you put a capital letter at the beginning of your
sentences and punctuation at the end?

Historical Figure Book

(Read 5 to 10 pages)

Title:_____Author:_____

Tell in your own words what you read.

_____

_____

_____

_____

_____

_____

_____

_____

_____

_____

A Time In History

After looking at pictures and learning about different people , places and things in history lets learn about dates in history.

Write Todays Date

_____

Look up what important thing happened in history on this day?

_____

_____

_____

Draw a picture of what happened.

Nature Study

Draw something in nature. Write one fact about your drawing.

_____

Math Time

Work in your math curriculum for 30 to 40 min.

Check when done. ___

Relax for a while and watch a tutorial or documentary for 30 min.

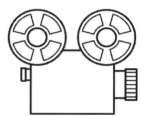 **Movie Review**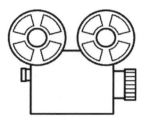

Write one thing you learned.

_____

Rate this movie. Color the stars.
5 stars mean it was Awesome!

Draw a scene from the movie.

Date :_____   Day 89

Bible Time

Read for 15 min. in your bible.

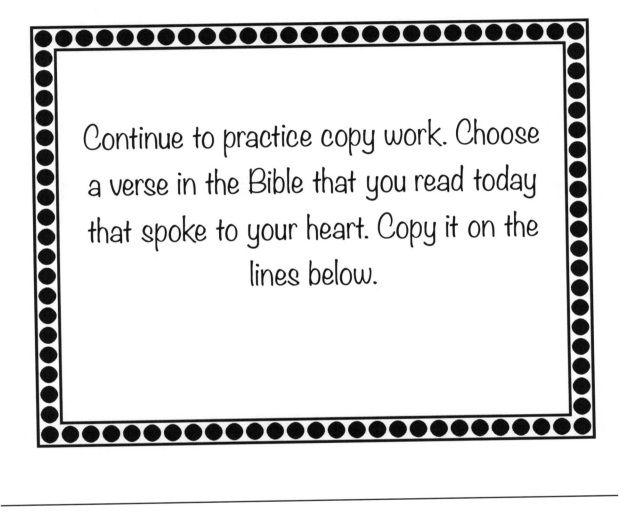

Continue to practice copy work. Choose a verse in the Bible that you read today that spoke to your heart. Copy it on the lines below.

_____

_____

_____

_____

_____

Reading and Language

Choose one of your classic novels to read.

(Read 5 pages)

Copy a paragraph from your book and circle all the adjectives.

Remember an adjective is a.....describing word !

_____

_____

_____

_____

_____

Did you put a capital letter at the beginning of your sentences and punctuation at the end?

Historical Figure Book

(Read 5 to 10 pages)

Title:_____Author:_____

Tell me about this persons character.

_____

_____

_____

Do you think this is a person you would like to be friends with?

_____

_____

_____

_____

_____

A Time In History

After looking at pictures and learning about different people , places and things in history lets learn about dates in history.

Write Todays Date

_____

Look up what important thing happened in history on this day?

_____

_____

_____

Draw a picture of what happened.

Nature Study

Draw something in nature. Write one fact about your drawing.

_____

Math Time

Work in your math curriculum for 30 to 40 min.

Check when done. ___

Relax for a while and watch a tutorial or documentary for 30 min.

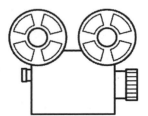 Movie Review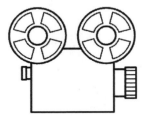

Write one thing you learned.

_____

Rate this movie. Color the stars.
5 stars mean it was Awesome!

Draw a scene from the movie.

Date : _____   Day 90

Bible Time

Read for 15 min. in your bible.

Continue to practice copy work. Choose a verse in the Bible that you read today that spoke to your heart. Copy it on the lines below.

_____

_____

_____

_____

_____

Reading and Language

Choose one of your classic novels to read.

(Read 5 pages)

Copy a paragraph from your book and circle all the nouns.

Remember a noun is a......person, place, thing, or idea !

_____

_____

_____

_____

_____

Did you put a capital letter at the beginning of your sentences and punctuation at the end?

Historical Figure Book

(Read 5 to 10 pages)

Title:_____ Author:_____

Do you think you could live during the time of your
historical figure? Tell why or why not.

_____

_____

_____

_____

_____

_____

_____

_____

_____

A Time In History

After looking at pictures and learning about different people , places and things in history lets learn about dates in history.

Write Todays Date

_____

Look up what important thing happened in history on this day?

_____

_____

_____

Draw a picture of what happened.

Nature Study

Draw something in nature. Write one fact about your drawing.

_____

Math Time

Work in your math curriculum for 30 to 40 min.

Check when done. ___

Relax for a while and watch a tutorial or documentary for 30 min.

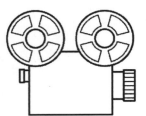 Movie Review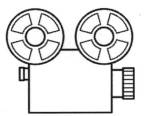

Write one thing you learned.

_____

Rate this movie. Color the stars.
5 stars mean it was Awesome!

Draw a scene from the movie.

Congratulations on finishing your 90 days of guided lessons!

To continue the school year begin book 2 of

A
Christian
Delight Directed
Curriculum

Once you have completed both books you will have finished 180 school days!

Date:_____

Parents signature:_____

<u>Copyright</u>

Made in United States
Orlando, FL
06 May 2022